G000151347

SMART CITIES, SMART FUTURE

SMART CITIES, SMART FUTURE

Showcasing Tomorrow

MIKE BARLOW
CORNELIA LÉVY-BENCHETON

WILEY

Copyright © 2019 by John Wiley & Sons, Inc. All rights reserved.

Published by John Wiley & Sons, Inc., Hoboken, New Jersey.
Published simultaneously in Canada.

No part of this publication may be reproduced, stored in a retrieval system, or
transmitted in any form or by any means, electronic, mechanical, photocopying,
recording, scanning, or otherwise, except as permitted under Section 107 or 108
of the 1976 United States Copyright Act, without either the prior written
permission of the Publisher, or authorization through payment of the appropriate
per-copy fee to the Copyright Clearance Center, Inc., 222 Rosewood Drive,
Danvers, MA 01923, (978) 750-8400, fax (978) 646-8600, or on the Web at www
.copyright.com. Requests to the Publisher for permission should be addressed to
the Permissions Department, John Wiley & Sons, Inc., 111 River Street, Hoboken,
NJ 07030, (201) 748-6011, fax (201) 748-6008, or online at www.wiley.com/go/
permissions.

Limit of Liability/Disclaimer of Warranty: While the publisher and author have used
their best efforts in preparing this book, they make no representations or
warranties with respect to the accuracy or completeness of the contents of this
book and specifically disclaim any implied warranties of merchantability or fitness
for a particular purpose. No warranty may be created or extended by sales
representatives or written sales materials. The advice and strategies contained
herein may not be suitable for your situation. You should consult with a
professional where appropriate. Neither the publisher nor author shall be liable for
any loss of profit or any other commercial damages, including but not limited to
special, incidental, consequential, or other damages.

For general information on our other products and services or for technical
support, please contact our Customer Care Department within the United States at
(800) 762-2974, outside the United States at (317) 572-3993, or fax (317) 572-4002.

Wiley publishes in a variety of print and electronic formats and by
print-on-demand. Some material included with standard print versions of this book
may not be included in e-books or in print-on-demand. If this book refers to media
such as a CD or DVD that is not included in the version you purchased, you may
download this material at http://booksupport.wiley.com. For more information
about Wiley products, visit www.wiley.com.

Library of Congress Cataloging-in-Publication Data is Available:

ISBN 9781119516187 (Hardcover)
ISBN 9781119516217 (ePDF)
ISBN 9781119516200 (ePub)

Cover Design: Burt Myers
Cover Image: © mikkelwilliam/iStockphoto

Printed in the United States of America

V10004633_091818

For Janine, Paul, and Elliot

CONTENTS

FOREWORD

Authors Mike Barlow and Cornelia Lévy-Bencheton have distilled hundreds of ideas, sources, technologies, and dreams into a thoughtful showcase of tomorrow. Much of the information is widely available, but their analysis, synthesis, and narrative make this a foundational guide for all of us.

And we need it.

Within the next 20 years, 70 percent of the world's population will be living in cities. The exponential change will be staggering. Designing and operating smarter cities is not just a movement—it is the inevitable shape of our future and the culture we are capable of building *together*. It will take an ecosystem—government, citizens, companies, and academics—to make sure that we do this right and hold each other accountable.

We have an opportunity to reimagine our cities and our lives in a way that is more equitable, more just, more sustainable, and just plain happier. But we need to do it *now* and make sure that new exponential technologies and governing bodies are of *service* and enhance the quality of life of our citizens.

As with all change, it will be uncomfortable. Citizens will demand transparency, higher levels of service, and quality of life. And they will be able to compare their services to their neighbors and to residents of other cities across the globe.

Today, lack of trust is one of the largest barriers to massive collaboration. We assume that each person and entity has an agenda. We've learned that it is hard to trust across borders or outside of our groups.

But one of the most exciting aspects of transformative technologies is the ability to delegate trust across decentralized networks. It will become much harder to incentivize people for actions that are not in the common interest. When we don't have to worry about trust, we can focus on what we can achieve. That level of collaboration has never been seen before and will be a powerful force in design and co-creation.

We are seeing an emerging cultural shift in which technology is the supportive tool set. The key questions are: How do we make tools that allow all of these cities and citizens to improve quality of life, and how do we scale citizen engagement and participation, so we can define and measure quality of life? That's what really matters.

Governments, private companies, and citizens will all need to work together to design these platforms, and to provide knowledge, outreach, and tools that are distributed, decentralized, and available to all. *The work that lies ahead is hard and it requires radical adaptability.*

As an entrepreneur, urbanist, and investor, I'm inspired by the seeds of the platforms outlined in this book. They speak to supporting citizens, citizen experience, and human-centered design. DigiTel, Tel Aviv's innovative citizen information platform, is a good example of the kind of people-focused technology we need. The goal of DigiTel is helping people to become more engaged with their city and its services. It helps residents form deeper and stronger emotional connections with the urban environment around them.

As a dreamer, I knew from the opening page that I would love this book. I don't think *Blade Runner*, I think Shambhala. If we imagine it, we can build it. And I nodded vigorously at every chapter, especially the book's opener...

> *El Dorado, Atlantis, Shambhala, Avalon, Xanadu, and Shangri-La. Those fabled places inspire our dreams. They are fantasies that nourish our imagination, spark our curiosity and embolden us to envision what could be... This book approaches the smart city from the perspective of the human spirit ... This is a book for dreamers and visionaries. We invite you to dream along with us and to imagine the world your children and grandchildren will inhabit.*

As a technologist, I know that our future urban systems will bridge data, provide insights, and be more efficient and transparent, but I feel a heavy responsibility to be a wise steward of these technologies and ensure that they are working for the people and designed with the people.

I started the US office of Waze nine years ago, underestimating the impact we would have on mobility and ultimately on city operations. One Friday night in 2012, I got a call from the White House during Superstorm Sandy. There was a fuel shortage on Staten Island, N.Y. Motorists were waiting in lines for three to four hours. The government asked for our help in collecting citizen data. For the first time ever, we sent a push notification to all Wazers in the area asking for information on which gas stations had power, which had fuel, and how long the lines were.

By the next day, we had thousands of responses that the Federal Emergency Management Agency (FEMA) could use to figure out where to send fuel trucks. That fundamentally changed my perception of what we were creating. It inspired the launch of the Waze Connected Citizens program to share data on incidents, traffic, events, and construction between Waze and city partners.

Since then, we've worked with over 650 cities, trying to help them use data as infrastructure. Our data has been used to improve emergency response times (e.g., in the United States, 70 percent of crashes are reported through Waze *before* they're reported through 911), close the loop on citizen problems, such as potholes and speed limit changes, redefine waste management and snowplow routes, and reduce congestion. In harnessing the insights of millions of Wazers, we have evolved from a traffic app to a change agent in traffic and mobility innovation.

One of our biggest successes came during the 2016 Summer Olympics in Rio de Janeiro. The city needed to accommodate a million visitors in an area that was already famously congested. We created an ad hoc team of Waze employees, Waze on-the-ground map editor volunteers, city officials, and citizens—all working together to collect and share the information as quickly as possible. The ad hoc partnerships performed marvelously, and case studies from Rio have now been shared with other cities, which can learn from these tests.

But we didn't stop there. We formed our Connected Citizens program with hundreds of global partners, including city, state, and national government agencies; nonprofits; and first responders. Software code from the program is now on GitHub and other open platforms, where it can be shared and adapted by cities and states all over the world.

Experiments are a start, but ongoing learning, iteration, operational tools, and transparency allow cities to become living laboratories in the best sense.

Based on this work, I'm now currently incubating new urban systems at Google's Area 120. Here are a few guiding motivations:

- Technology can enable cultures to flourish in their own unique ways.

- Technology should remove unwanted friction and allow people to focus on quality of life.

- Technology must evolve hand in hand with ethics, philosophy, and society.

- Technology is the best opportunity we have to discover the needs, ideas, and voices of every citizen.

I look at this as a move toward the self-awareness of cities. Self-awareness describes a process of learning, reflecting, acting on what we've learned, and constant adaptation to become better. A city is a living organism that adapts with every new citizen, event, visitor, and policy.

A city can have its own self-awareness, powered by technology in service of society. Self-awareness is also a cornerstone of a life well lived for individuals within a community. We will screw things up, we will scrap ideas that sounded good and were voted in. We will iterate and learn.

Self-awareness is the most human of goals. We want to improve, see things clearly, and understand our place in the world. This is what the right urban technology platform and planning can enable.

Existential technologies, including robots, artificial intelligence (AI), blockchains, and even self-driving cars, can fundamentally alter society and must be deployed thoughtfully and responsibly as part of an entire intelligent system. We will need to deal with issues, such as privacy in blockchain, bias in AI, fair economic development in robotics, and just use of space, as well as other important policy decisions.

The goal of this effort is the wise stewardship of technology to support culture and society through a new urban system that is dynamic, adaptive, and supportive.

I read this manuscript while in Barcelona, Spain, a city that was referenced multiple times for its quality of support and civic engagement. I was inspired to visit projects and places mentioned by authors Mike and Cornelia, such as the Institute of Advanced Architecture of Catalonia, where they are 3D printing algorithmic "bricks" of local soil and crafting citizen sensor kits.

I see technology being used to make tools to be used by all. Developed at Barcelona's Laboratory for Democratic Innovation, Decidim is a joint effort of 17 organizations, including software companies, industry consortiums, research institutions, and civic associations. Decidim allows citizens to propose ideas, conduct surveys, call public meetings, and join the debate on whether proposals are good solutions to identified needs. Decidim is currently used by municipalities in other parts of Spain, and by local governments in Finland and France.

For me, this book is a call to action. As they say in Catalonia: *Decidem*. We decide. Let's get on it!

Di-Ann Eisnor
Director Area 120, Google

ACKNOWLEDGMENTS

Smart Cities, Smart Future is our interpretation of a global phenomenon that is rapidly transforming our lives. The book is both a distillation of our research and a window into the future of our planet.

The book also includes a glossary of essential smart-city terms and supplementary lists of worthwhile conferences and strong organizations making a difference in the worldwide smart-city movement.

Smart cities are complex blends of interoperable technologies, systems, and services designed and orchestrated to help people lead productive, fulfilling, safe, and happy lives.

No two smart cities are alike. No one can say with certainty or precision what the term "smart city" means. Clearly, the smart-city movement is a work in progress. There is no standard definition or template.

We have done our best, however, to capture and convey the depth and richness of the smart-city movement, and to explain its potential as a force for positive change.

We take a human-centered approach to the subject, describing the impact of smart-city projects on people in towns, cities, and nations around the world. The book includes descriptions of ongoing smart-city projects in North America, Europe, Asia, and the Middle East.

As you will see in the chapters ahead, we are more interested in people than in technology. In a very real sense, this book is the story of smart citizens whose lives are transformed by smart-city projects, initiatives, and programs. The book is a guide to an emerging world in which people interact continuously with smart machines, vehicles, buildings, and systems.

Smart Cities, Smart Future is a combination of research and journalism. In addition to studying the subject in exhaustive detail, we interviewed dozens of experts and active participants in the smart-city movement. At the end of the book, we have included short biographies of the sources we interviewed at length and quoted directly.

For sharing their knowledge, time, and energy, we are profoundly grateful to the following people: Hannes Astok, Xabier E. Barandiaran, Jeffrey J. Blatt, Francesca Bria, Boyd Cohen, Di-Ann Eisnor, Andrew Guthrie Ferguson, Christina Franken, Pete Herzog, Mike Holland, Kevin Fan Hsu, Jerry MacArthur Hultin, Jon Jennings, Ariel Kennan, Matthew Klein, Martin Kõiva, Alan Leidner, I-Ping Li, Josh Lieberman, Amen Ra Mashariki, Dale W. Meyerrose, Chris Moschovitis, Emma Mulqueeny, Joseph Okpaku, Gala Pin, Jake Porway, Vijay Raja, Jennifer Robinson, Jennifer Sanders, Eytan Schwartz, Leah Shahum, Zohar Sharon, Dave Shuman, Lisa Smith, Kirk Steudle, Linnar Viik, and James Von Klemperer.

We also thank Morey Altman, Edith Barlow, Michael Batty, Dominique Bonte, Laura Brumley, Barry Coflan, Pilar

Conesa, Joe Cortright, Kate Daly, Robby Demming, Luc De Rooms, Leila Dillon, Lisa Faison, Paul Feiner, Gordon Feller, Ari Gesher, Julie Kerr, Meeli Kõiva, Erin Kuller, Michael Lake, Julia Ingrid Lane, Richard Laudor, Mike Loukides, Areti Markopoulou, Alex Mateo, Roger Millar, Cathy O'Neil, Paula Paige, Edna Pasher, Jonathan Reichental, Natalia Rivas, Euan Semple, Sapan Shah, Sameer Sharma, Ian Slesser, Richard Soley, Debbe Stern, Kirk Steudle, Judith Urbano, Melinda Venable, Noreen Whysel, Miriam Young, and Diana Zitnay for their suggestions, feedback, assistance, and advice.

We offer special thanks to our good friends at bee smart city—Thomas Müller, Bart Gorynski, and Alexander Gelsin—for their generous contributions to our chapter on the stages of smart-city evolution and development.

Additionally, we thank our editor, Sheck Cho, and his assistant editor, Michael Henton, for their guidance and support throughout the project.

We wrote this book with you, the reader, in mind. We hope you find it informative, educational, and enjoyable. We wish you good health, long life, and great adventures.

INTRODUCTION

Thomas Müller

Co-founder and managing partner at bee smart city

What is a smart city? The term itself is a sticky concept in a slippery environment. Most of its definitions revolve around technology and data science.

Unquestionably, technology and data science are critical enablers, but the outcome depends less on the enablers themselves than on how they are applied. What works in the laboratory doesn't necessarily work in real life.

The smartest smart-city solutions target specific groups within a city or a community. They engage directly with citizens and users to generate benefits that can be readily appreciated and understood. Building a smart city is an ongoing endeavor of development, design, implementation, adoption, feedback, iteration, and continuous improvement.

A smart city helps people imagine and create solutions for improving "the place we call home."[1] A smart city provides its residents with the capabilities and resources they need to find happiness, fulfillment, and prosperity.

It cannot be a purely top-down process. Smart cities arise from people working together to achieve common goals. In other words, it's a team effort.

Boyd Cohen, a researcher, author, and visionary entrepreneur, describes three levels, or generations, of the smart cities movement:[2]

Smart cities 1.0: Technology Driven

Smart cities 2.0: Technology Enabled, City Led

Smart cities 3.0: Citizen Co-created

Smart cities don't evolve in lockstep. Cities follow different evolutionary paths, each at its own pace. The smartest smart cities have reached the third level, in which citizens work together to develop solutions that genuinely matter to them, rather than relying primarily on vendors or consultants.

Collaboration Engines

A smart city is an ecosystem of people, processes, and solutions. The most important driver of success is collective effort—the sum of many individual actions taken in pursuit of a shared goal.

In a very real and concrete fashion, smart cities serve as collaboration engines. In the parlance of the software industry, they are platforms. They provide a common hub for individuals, and for groups, organizations, agencies, and companies.

Cities all over the world have recognized the benefits of becoming smarter. The term "smart city" began as a trendy catchphrase that was used somewhat indiscriminately by technology marketers. Today, smart cities are a global phenomenon with real staying power.

Focused on People

We are especially pleased to see the adoption of human-centric approaches to engaging citizens and other stakeholders early in the process of smart-city solution development, as well as in later trial and roll-out phases.

Human-centric approaches are absolutely imperative. Simply unveiling a new municipal service won't convince people to use it—they need to understand how it will help them.

Smart cities encourage bottom-up innovation and co-creation. At a very deep level, they understand that building a smart city is a democratic process. They also recognize and appreciate the emergence of "smartivists," a term for individual citizens who actively promote or support smart-city initiatives on a voluntary basis.

Smartivists play an important part in the smart-city movement by offering their expertise, energy, and experience. They can work as individuals or in groups. Sometimes they help by establishing or leading coalitions of stakeholders focused on solving specific problems in their city or community. They represent a new and exciting form of civic activism.

Additionally, smartivists become a valuable source of collective intelligence and hands-on knowledge. Their combination of commitment, enthusiasm and local pride bring vitality and a sense of continuity to the smart-city movement.[3]

Dealing with Obstacles

It would be pleasant to imagine that smart cities won't face problems, but that would be an unrealistic hope. There are still barriers, pitfalls, and traps for the unwary. Some cities will opt for quick technology fixes, instead of finding ways to harness the collective energy of their citizens to identify, prioritize, and solve problems.

Data ownership, privacy, and security will become major issues as people become more generally aware of the risks associated with continual surveillance and monitoring. Those concerns must be taken seriously; they can't simply be swept under the rug or kicked down the road. Smart cities will doubtlessly be at the front lines of any battles over data collection and data usage.

The digital divide is often forgotten when people talk about new technology, but it's a real problem that must be confronted. How will cities guarantee that all residents—regardless of age, education, social, or health status—are served fairly and equitably?

Will Government Help or Hinder?

City governments have highly complex structures and they tick in certain ways. Politics, budgetary constraints, legacy systems, and traditional modes of thinking can easily slow down or even derail the development of smart-city projects.

The development of smart cities and communities requires strong leadership and a long-term vision. For some people, the idea of getting involved in local government might seem like a waste of time.

Most government officials want to help, and they are open to ideas from their constituents. They might not move as quickly as you would like them to, but they will move eventually.

Don't use government inertia as an excuse for not participating. If smart cities are important to you, attend a public meeting at your local town or village hall and make your voice heard. You will be surprised at how easy it is to participate in the process and to make a difference.

Connected Ecosystems

We recommend thinking about smart cities in holistic terms and remembering that cities exist within larger regional ecosystems. Cities are not remote islands; they are physically and digitally connected with the rest of the world. Smart cities are part of a global community, so there's no need for going it alone.

There are hundreds of smart cities to learn from. We urge you to visit some of them—especially if you want to become a smartivist. If you can't afford to travel, use a web browser or a smartphone to find out what people are doing in smart cities. It's amazing how much useful information about smart cities can be gleaned from online searching.

Here's an extremely abbreviated list of smart cities that are worth learning more about. Taking a look at these cities will get you off to a good start:

Europe

Amsterdam (Netherlands)

Barcelona (Spain)

Copenhagen (Denmark)

Eindhoven (Netherlands)

Espoo (Finland)

Nice (France)

Vienna (Austria)

The Americas

Columbus, Ohio (US)

Kansas City, Missouri (US)

Mexico City (Mexico)

New York (US)

Palo Alto, California (US)

Portland, Oregon (US)

Rio de Janeiro (Brazil)

San Diego, California (US)

Seattle, Washington (US)

Middle East, Asia, and Asia-Pacific

Adelaide (Australia)

Bhubaneswar (India)

Dubai (United Arab Emirates)

Meixi Lake (China)

Melbourne (Australia)

Moscow (Russia)

Singapore

Tel Aviv (Israel)

Wuxi (China)

Yinchan (China)

In addition to reading this book and visiting the bee smart city website, we recommend downloading the Global Smart City Performance Index[4] created for Intel by Juniper Research. The index ranks smart cities across four dimensions: mobility, health care, public safety, and productivity.

Setting the Stage for Long-Term Success

Establishing an ecosystem of human-centric solutions over time sets the stage for long-term success and takes smart cities to the next level in their journey toward becoming models for all cities.

Not all solutions need to be homegrown. Municipalities should look beyond their borders and the borders of their regions for existing solutions that can be replicated or adapted for local use. Learning from other cities and communities, and sharing best practices, is an integral part of the smart-city journey.

Platforms for Continuous Innovation

We believe that smart cities have the potential to become the world's leading platforms for continuous innovation in areas such as public safety, public health, mobility, education, finance, trade, immigration, energy efficiency, waste management, cybersecurity, data science, robotics, and many other critical domains of modern life.

At bee smart city, we're doing our part to support the development of smarter cities by providing a global platform for adaptable and replicable smart-city solutions that have been implemented successfully in hundreds of cities around the world.[5] On our platform, we connect thousands of government users, solution providers, research, and university specialists—as well as smartivists—so they can take their cities and communities forward. On our global hub, we share successful smart-city strategies and solutions as well as city case studies that provide added value for smart-city development.[6]

Success in smart cities essentially is a result of knowledge and experience drawn from external and internal collective intelligence combined in local collaborative and purposeful actions. Or as we say at bee smart city, "Be a bee." Bees are known for their willingness to work together, collaborate and contribute to the common good of the hive. Let's follow their example as we pioneer the new world of smart cities.

Endnotes

1. https://hub.beesmart.city/strategy/a-review-of-becoming-a-smart-city

2. https://www.fastcompany.com/3047795/the-3-generations-of-smart-cities

3. https://hub.beesmart.city/strategy/towards-a-new-paradigm-of-the-smart-city

4. https://newsroom.intel.com/wp-content/uploads/sites/11/2018/03/smart-cities-whats-in-it-for-citizens.pdf

5. https://www.beesmart.city

6. https://hub.beesmart.city

Chapter 1

Cities of Our Dreams

EL DORADO, Atlantis, Shambhala, Avalon, Xanadu, and Shangri-La. Those fabled places inspire our dreams. They are fantasies that nourish our imagination, spark our curiosity, and embolden us to envision what could be.

The smart city is a modern myth, a dream for our time. It's an archetype and an ideal, formed in the realm of our collective unconscious. It's a magical place we long for, a vision shimmering in the distance and yet embedded deeply in our psyche.

For those of us who love cities, the smart city is where we want to live, work, play, raise a family, start a business, or simply stroll around on a pleasant day. The smart city inspires genius and originality. It also offers tranquility and peace.

This book approaches the smart city from the perspective of the human spirit. In the chapters ahead, you will learn about people using technology, rather than about technology itself.

This is a book for dreamers and visionaries. We invite you to dream along with us and to imagine the world your children and grandchildren will inhabit.

Today, more than half of the world's population lives in cities. The most urbanized regions of the world are North America (82 percent of the population lives in urban areas), Latin America and the Caribbean (81 percent), Europe (74 percent), and Oceania (68 percent). Africa remains mostly rural, with only 43 percent of its population living in cities.

About half of the population of Asia now lives in cities. That proportion will surely grow as Asian economies modernize and expand. Asia is still comparatively rural, but that won't be the case for much longer.

Inescapably, we are becoming an urban planet. From 1950 to 2018, the urban population jumped from 751 million to 4.2 billion. By midcentury, two-thirds of us will be urbanites. Cities will grow in size and scale; by 2030, the world will have more than 43 megacities with populations of at least 10 million.[1] Clearly, the world of tomorrow will be a world of cities (Figure 1.1).

Urbanization is not a new trend; people have been migrating to cities for millennia. What's changed? The velocity of migration has accelerated significantly. "Three or four thousand years ago, you needed an oxcart and a brave heart

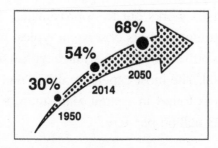

Figure 1.1 Global urban population growth
Source: Population Division of the Department of Economic and Social Affairs of the United Nations, World Urbanization Prospects: The 2018 Revision (New York: United Nations, 16 May 2018).

to make the arduous journey from the hinterlands to the nearest walled settlement," we wrote in *Smart Cities, Smarter Citizens*. "Today, you can take an airplane from practically anywhere and arrive at the city of your choice in hours."[2]

What *hasn't* changed? The basic socioeconomic drivers are the same. For as long as there have been cities, city living has been considered a step up from the countryside. Cities offer more economic opportunities, higher standards of living, more services, better health, and more access to culture than rural communities.[3] That's why people move to cities.

In addition to being generators of wealth, cities possess intrinsic value. Small patches of urban real estate are worth much more than similar patches of land in rural or suburban areas. For investors, city land is a hot commodity.

A detailed study by economists at the University of Illinois and the University of Michigan estimated that 76,581 square miles of urban land in the United States is worth roughly

$25 trillion. That works out to approximately $511,000 per acre. As the study's authors observe, a typical fifth-acre residential lot is worth about $100,000 and a typical parking space is worth $2,000. The most expensive urban real estate in the United States is found in central Manhattan, where land is valued at $123 million per acre.[4]

Part of the reason for the sky-high value of city land is simple economics: The demand for urban space is rising, and the supply of urban space is limited by physical constraints.

The high cost of urban real estate is also driven by desire. Cities work on our emotions and excite our passions. They are magnets for people and businesses; they offer intangible benefits that generations of poets, songwriters, and novelists have tried to capture.

In *The Warhol Economy,* Elizabeth Currid observes how cities "attract the human capital that drives the economy." Currid's book focuses on New York City, yet her insight can be applied globally. In addition to providing ample opportunities for face-to-face contact, cities offer "dense networks of both collaboration and competition" that are necessary for maintaining strong and vibrant economies.

Cities provide the critical mass necessary for generating life-altering opportunities and learning experiences. When we confront other human beings, make eye contact and engage with strangers, we become sharper, smarter, and more confident. That's why city folk often seem to have an "edge." We're proud of our abilities to discern instantly between someone who is merely odd and someone who is potentially dangerous.

Metropolitan habitats provide the vital sparks that enliven our existences. Jon Jennings, the city manager of Portland, Maine, calls the city's quality of life its "secret sauce." When Portland decided to use advanced technologies, such as radar sensors and artificial intelligence to reduce traffic congestion, its goal was improving the lives of its residents and making it easier for tourists who support the local economy to navigate city streets.

For Jennings, the smart-city movement is about rebuilding trust in government and providing better municipal services. It's also about helping cities adjust to the needs and expectations of a new generation.

"We're all busier. We all lead active lives. We would all prefer to have fewer hassles," Jennings says. "Today, we have expectations that we can get things done immediately, or at least more rapidly than was possible in the past. When we apply new technologies in Portland, we're doing it to make people's lives easier."

What Makes a City Smart?

What is a *smart* city and how is it different from our traditional notion of a city? There is no single definition for a smart city. The term itself is a moving target; no one can agree on exactly what it means.

At minimum, it's a technologically enabled version of what urban activist and writer Jane Jacobs described as a "fantastically dynamic" place, a "fertile ground" for millions of people who hope and plan for better lives.

A smart city encourages people to walk, meet, talk, and congregate on streets, in shops, and in public spaces. It's a place where people interact easily, effortlessly, and joyfully with each other and with their environment. It's a place of random informal interactions, serendipitous meetings, and spontaneous relationships.

Most of all, it's a place where people feel safe—not because they are surrounded by cops and cameras, but because the city's cyber-physical infrastructure is designed intentionally for the purpose of creating an atmosphere of trust, community and shared responsibility.

Smart cities make it easy for people to travel from one neighborhood to another. They provide a mix of transportation solutions that reduce traffic congestion and diminish harmful emissions from vehicles.

They provide seamless broadband and Wi-Fi coverage. In a smart city, there are no dead zones and no dropped calls. Free charging stations are conveniently placed; no one worries about the batteries in their phones dying.

Smart cities take energy efficiency to the next level; they generate more power than they consume. Smart cities grow their own food and manufacture products from recycled materials. They measure water usage by the drop and conserve natural resources by the ton. They're miserly, yet in a good way—in a smart city, nothing goes to waste.

Smart cities have solar-powered smart trash bins that signal when they're getting full. That might not seem like a big deal, but smart trash bins save cities millions of dollars annually by reducing the costs of collecting garbage.

Smart cities have smart streetlights equipped with sensors that spot potholes, measure traffic flow, listen for gunshots, and help drivers find empty parking spaces.

They have smart systems that make it easy for citizens to obtain permits and licenses without having to stand in line at city hall. They remove the friction and complexity from processes, such as paying taxes, registering children for school, and finding health care for an aging parent.

Cities on a Hill

There's a lot more to smart cities than fixing potholes and providing excellent broadband coverage. Smart cities are living laboratories. They are role models and exemplars. They are explorers and pioneers, navigating a course for the future of humankind.

Smart cities deal head on with thorny modern problems, such as transportation, energy efficiency, education, public safety, public health, citizen engagement, privacy, immigration, economic inequality, climate change, and cybersecurity.

are problems that cannot be sidestepped, down-
played, or delegated to higher authorities. In many instances,
cities and towns have little choice but to step up and create
their own solutions. They must do or die.

Smart cities are co-synchronous with *new localism*, a
movement based on the belief that many problems are best
solved at local levels. That might not seem like a particularly
revolutionary idea, yet it's a significant departure from the
20th-century maxim that big government is the answer to all
problems, large and small.

Today, the methods of big government are under attack.
There's been a shift in thinking, especially in the realm
of problem solving. In the decades following World War
II, urban planning methods reflected the era's bias for
command-and-control hierarchies. Plain-vanilla projects that
neither pleased nor offended anyone were built in cities all
over the world.

Much of the urban planning from that era was based
on a shaky foundation of misconceptions and prejudices.
It assumed that crowded streets were bad, that cars were good,
and that poor people should live in soul-crushing, high-rise
apartment projects. Postwar urban planning was epitomized
by legendary figures, such as Robert Moses and Le Corbusier,
who sought to eliminate the natural chaos of city life and
replace it with something more orderly and manageable.

That postwar approach emphasized grand scale and epic
proportions. It assumed that if a project was important, it must
be big—and if a project was big, it must be important. That

kind of circular reasoning was used to justify decades of bad urban planning.

For cities, smallness is an asset. Cities are naturally limited in size, which turns out to be an advantage. They don't have to solve problems on a huge scale. They don't have to devise enormous projects. They can afford to think small.

Most of the projects we describe in this book are practical, functional, and human centered. Some of them involve amazing feats of technological prowess, although many of them are small and simple. Several are built on the ruins of previous ideas that failed because they were too grand or too far ahead of their time.

A New Approach to City Planning

Smart cities are beneficiaries of a new method of urban planning that emphasizes collaboration, co-creation, crowd-sourcing, and grassroots efforts. The new method combines bottom-up innovation with cross-functional insight to create entirely fresh and original solutions for complex problems. It focuses less on grand strategy and more on tactical solutions.

The new method is informed and influenced by software development techniques, such as Agile and DevOps, and by design thinking, a process that starts by exploring the problems of people in the real world and working backward to develop practical solutions. The new method uses rapid lightweight prototyping, pilot projects, pop-ups, and virtual reality to evaluate, refine, and continuously improve ideas before they're launched.

The new method is firmly rooted in data science, which allows cities to rigorously test new ideas and predict in advance which are most likely to succeed in the real world.

Smart cities use data science to determine the size and location of pocket parks, playgrounds, sidewalk extensions, community gardens, pedestrian malls, bike paths, and traffic circles. Instead of simply guessing where those amenities are needed, smart cities use data to generate predictive models—and then they test the accuracy of the models before moving forward.

Thinking beyond Technology

Smart cities of the 21st century are enabled by modern digital technologies; that is a given. Technology alone, however, doesn't make a city smart. The technology must be fully integrated and deeply woven into the fabric of the city. It can't be an afterthought or a thinly applied veneer. It must be an active component, thoroughly baked into the city's infrastructure and inseparable from the daily experiences of city life.

Technology isn't something bolted on at the last minute, it must be part of an overall solution designed to meet the needs of people. Imagining, designing, building, and managing smart cities is an interdisciplinary effort requiring input from experts and stakeholders from multiple industries and economic sectors.

"It takes more than just cramming technology into cities," says Kevin Fan Hsu, co-founder of the Human Cities Initiative at Stanford University. "It takes intelligent planning to build cities that are responsive and adaptive. Cities are communities of human beings with distinct needs, hopes, and aspirations. Today, urban design arises from collaboration with communities. It's no longer a top-down vision imposed from above."

Smart cities follow the basic principles of design thinking and human-centered design, which prioritize the needs of people and use science to guide the development of projects. Smart cities favor neighborhood initiatives over grandiose master plans; they know the quality of life in a city depends on healthy streets, vibrant shops, and a diversified economy.

Looking Backward

When we think of smart cities, we tend to think in futuristic terms. We often use the language and iconography of futurism to express our visions of what a smart city should look like. But we should also look to the past for lessons and examples of how previous generations handled the challenges of planning and developing urban spaces.

In the mid-19th century, Baron Georges-Eugène Haussmann transformed Paris from a medieval collection of sprawling neighborhoods into one of the world's first genuinely modern cities. He used the tools and techniques of his day—parks, public squares, large monuments, axial roadways, sewers, water-distribution systems, and standard cornice lines—to complete the city's transformation (Figure 1.2).

At roughly the same time, Ildefons Cerdà, who coined the term "urbanism," was planning the expansion of Barcelona. Cerdà designed an orthogonal grid for the city's new streets,

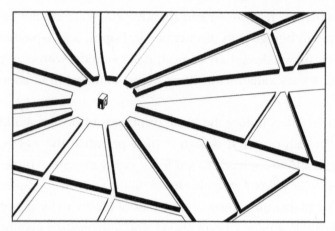

Figure 1.2 Radial street design in Paris
Source: Burt Myers.

which created a sense of order and clarity. He also had the sidewalks cut at a 45-degree angle at street intersections (known as "chamfered corners"), an innovation that created mini plazas with shops and services all over the new part of the city (Figure 1.3). Cerdà was a transportation expert, and

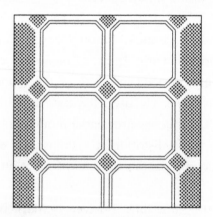

Figure 1.3 Chamfered corners in Barcelona
Source: Burt Myers.

he planned the streets and avenues of the expansion with traffic in mind.

Visionary planners such as Haussmann and Cerdà serve as vivid reminders that smart cities are created by smart people. Both men had a deep understanding of the cities they were tasked with redesigning, and they used the tools at hand to bring their visions to life.

In today's cities, "smart" and "high-tech" are not necessarily synonymous. Most smart-city projects don't require advanced degrees in engineering or terabytes of computing power. Our research shows the primary requirements for creating successful smart-city projects are deep knowledge of local problems, imaginative thinking, thorough research, good planning, bold action, and persistent follow-through.

Bicycle-sharing services in Madrid, 100 miles of running trails in Portland, Oregon, banning automobile traffic in New York's Central Park, and providing free public transit in Tallinn, Estonia, are all examples of smart-city projects driven primarily by local governments or community groups responding to the needs of citizens. In most cases, technology is an enabler, not a motivator.

Smart by Necessity

The island of Singapore learned early that it could lever-age science to control its destiny. Formed as an independent republic in 1965, the industrious city-nation is home to more than 5.9 million people.[5] Singapore has few sources of fresh water and depends on nearby Malaysia for most of its drinking water. That's a problem because Singapore's contract to import water from Malaysian state of Johor expires in 2061. By then, water demand in Singapore will have roughly doubled from its present level of 430 million gallons per day.

Soon after its formation, Singapore began experimenting with water reclamation to produce "industrial water," which is nonpotable water used by businesses. Singapore's experiments have since blossomed, resulting in an ongoing series of innovative techniques and processes for reclaiming water, ranging from desalination of seawater to meticulous recycling and rain catchment. "We attempt to catch every drop of rain that falls in Singapore," Peter Joo Hee Ng, chief executive of PUB, Singapore's national water agency, told Nick Michell of *The Source*.[6]

In 2003, following many years of experimentation and development, Singapore introduced NEWater to the public. NEWater is ultraclean water recycled from treated sewage in a "rigorous three-step purification process involving ultrafiltration/microfiltration, reverse osmosis (RO), and ultraviolet (UV) disinfection," according to an article published by the World Economic Forum.[7]

NEWater is pumped into the city's reservoirs, where it's mixed with rainwater before being treated and made available for direct consumption. Singapore expects water from its NEWater and desalination plants to meet up to 85 percent of its future water needs.[8]

Meantime, Singapore isn't standing still. The city-nation continues to refine its water processing capabilities, and sends promising students to doctoral programs where they can learn the newest techniques for treating and reclaiming "used" water.[9]

By necessity, Singapore has become a global leader in water reclamation science. Yet water purification is only one of many areas in which the city-nation applies innovative technologies to help its citizens.

With ongoing projects for improving and transforming health care, transportation, education, public safety, housing, and elder care, Singapore is justly called the "smartest of smart cities." It's also consistently ranked among the top nations in the Human Development Index,[10] a data-driven study produced annually by the United Nations.

Singapore's careful calibration of the social, economic, and physical needs of its residents is a key part of its remarkable success as a nation and a city.

Public-Private Partnerships

Smart-city planning depends on strong and healthy relationships between the private and public sectors. "Planning should be defined as public action that generates a sustained and widespread private reaction," writes Alexander Garvin in *The American City: What Works, What Doesn't*.

As Garvin correctly observes, a project cannot be considered successful unless it has a positive impact on the community around it. Cities are complex amalgams of public and commercial enterprises; smart-city initiatives must be designed with both constituencies in mind. Many of the examples described in this book are the results of public-private partnerships, which are absolutely essential to the development of smart cities.

Public-private partnership is not a new idea. New York City's first subway system was a public-private partnership. Haussmann's rebuilding of Paris was financed through public-private partnerships.

In addition to providing alternative methods for raising capital, public-private partnerships can accelerate the pace of developing and implementing smart-city projects. The Dallas Innovation Alliance, for example, has successfully launched nine projects in the city's West End District, a historic neighborhood that had experienced a deep economic downturn in the early 2000s.

The alliance focuses on gathering data and presenting it to city officials to speed their decision-making processes. "We try to get all the players together in a room and we take a 'best minds' approach to solving problems," explains Jennifer Sanders, co-founder and executive director of the alliance. "As a free-standing nonprofit, we're able to move quickly. We don't get caught in the shuffle that often slows down projects. One of our main roles is providing evidence that justifies larger-scale deployments of smart-city projects."

In 2017, the alliance created the Smart Cities Living Lab for the West End district. The lab is a test bed for smart-city initiatives, providing a transparent and repeatable process for evaluating projects. One of its most successful projects was the installation of small beacons that measured pedestrian traffic in the district.

"We were able to measure foot traffic and share the information with members of the local business association. The beacons revealed unexpected spikes in pedestrian traffic, which enabled local businesses to adjust their hours and tweak their marketing to attract more customers," Sanders says.

Another project involved replacing the district's sodium halide streetlamps with light-emitting diodes (LEDs). In addition to saving energy and increasing safety, the lights can be controlled remotely.

"There's a popular restaurant in the district with a patio. One of the new streetlights was shining directly on the patio, making patrons uncomfortable. We called the city, explained the situation and they reduced the intensity of the light by 30 percent," Sanders recalls. "Some cities have had situations where streetlights were shining into apartment buildings, making it difficult for residents to sleep. With the LEDs, cities can dial down the intensity, allowing people to sleep better at night."

The LEDs send signals when they're broken or in need of replacement, which reduces the amount of time city inspectors spend looking for broken bulbs. The new LEDs lower the city's labor and fuel costs, and diminish the city's carbon footprint.

The aggregate impact of the Living Lab has been positive, Sanders says. Residents and visitors to the West End feel safer and more connected, local businesses are serving more customers, and the district's spirit has become noticeably more upbeat.

"Public-private partnerships are becoming increasingly critical at the city level," Sanders says. "They help cities move initiatives quickly and implement high-value infrastructure projects at city scale, without relying on traditional approaches." The goal, she says, is executing projects that involve limited upfront capital expenditures, which then allows cities to focus on optimizing operations.

PPPs, as they are called, are emerging as essential components of smart-city development. In the past, financing capital projects required cities to borrow large sums of money, usually by issuing municipal bonds. PPPs allow cities to leverage private capital without the encumbrances and delays associated with traditional methods of municipal financing.

Open Data

Open data, which is any kind of public data that can be easily downloaded and analyzed by any groups or individuals, also plays an important role in smart cities. Open data includes building permits, unsealed court records, real estate trans-actions, government spending, water usage, air quality, and census data.

Vision Zero, a global project for eliminating all traffic fatal-ities,[11] relies primarily on the rigorous analysis of public data on traffic accidents. Smart cities in Europe and North America use Vision Zero strategies to make streets and roads safer for walking, cycling, and driving (Figure 1.4).

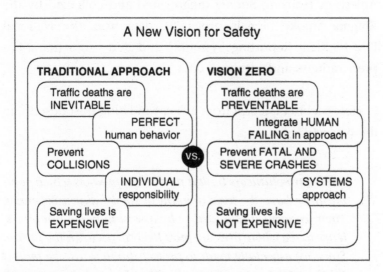

Figure 1.4 Vision Zero strategy for reducing traffic fatalities
Source: Vision Zero.

Open data is also reducing deaths from home fires in the United States, where three of every five home-fire deaths occur in homes with no smoke alarms or no working smoke alarms.[12] In Washington, D.C., data scientists from DataKind, a global nonprofit based in Brooklyn, New York, partnered with the American Red Cross to develop the Home Fire

Risk Map,[13] an online resource that targets high-risk homes for smoke alarm installations and fire-safety education.

The map began with a DataDive—a weekend during which volunteers from DataKind partner with a nonprofit to solve a problem. In this case, dozens of DataKind DC volunteers partnered with eight American Red Cross staffers on what eventually became a yearlong project fueled by open data from the American Community Survey and the American Housing Survey (aggregated and collected by the Enigma Smoke Signals project[14]), data from the National Fire Incident Reporting System,[15] and Red Cross home-fire preparedness and response data.

Here's a brief excerpt from a DataKind blog post describing the project:[16]

> *First, our volunteers built a model that predicts which communities have the least amount of smoke-alarm coverage. Then we went a step further by assessing home-fire prevalence to see where fires are most likely to occur in the future. Since we especially want to protect inhabitants, we built a third model that predicts the likelihood of an injury or death when a home fire does occur. All of these models are encapsulated within the Home Fire Risk Map.*

Organizations, such as DataKind—which has chapters in Bangalore, San Francisco, Singapore, the UK, and Washington, D.C.,—are key players in an emerging ecosystem of people, processes, and technologies supporting the smart-city movement.

They also represent a new style of hands-on citizen engagement and civic commitment occurring at the grassroots level. For years, community activists have held bake sales, car washes, rallies, and parades. In smart cities, they'll also hold hackathons, coding fairs, and DataDives.

Skin in the Game

Smart cities are at the vanguard of the new approach to solving urban problems. They are far more flexible, agile, and responsive than national governments. If there are solutions to the world's hardest problems, smart cities will find them first.

In almost every imaginable way, smart cities are the antidote to the rigidly planned cities of the mid-20th century: cities in which high-rise towers surrounded by dead space spawned ghostly neighborhoods where citizens dared not tread after dark.

"The physical and the social are deeply connected in cities," write Richard Sennett and Ricky Burdett in their preface to *The Quito Papers and the New Urban Agenda*. That connection was broken by principles of urban planning conceived in the 1930s and applied relentlessly for the next six decades.

The smart-city movement redirects the trajectory of urban planning. Smart cities are platforms for a new kind of urban development. They put the tools and techniques of planning into the hands of more people, giving them skin in the game.

They also empower a new generation of architects whose toolbox now includes software for visualizing the complex interplay between buildings and their surrounding environments in greater detail than ever before.

Even as design and construction techniques evolve, architecture will continue to shape the destiny of cities. Smart-city architecture is likely to reflect the fluid and turbulent nature of modern life. Architectural development will be iterative—a nonstop journey of experimentation, feedback, refinement, and innovation. The forms and structures around us will create what Sennett describes as "a strong sense of a process unfolding."[17]

While it is unlikely that we'll see "agile" architecture any time soon, the idea of adaptability has become increasingly relevant for urban architects and their firms. "It's hard to change the basic form of an existing building. But the best buildings are adaptable to new uses," says James Von Klemperer, president and design principal at Kohn Pedersen Fox Associates.

Adaptable buildings don't need to be torn down when the society around them changes. In Manhattan, for example, some of the trendiest neighborhoods are in former warehouse districts. In addition to being ruggedly built, the old warehouses had spacious floors, high ceilings, and broad proportions—making them perfect spaces for galleries, lofts, and stores. The buildings remained essentially unchanged, even as their function evolved into something completely new.

"These buildings are sustainable...we can reuse them and avoid the cycle of constant rebuilding that is destructive to the planet," Von Klemperer says. "They are 'agile' in the sense that they allow different activities to flow through them."

Ideally, smart cities would require buildings to be designed and constructed with adaptability in mind. For instance, cities could set higher minimums for floor-to-ceiling heights when new parking garages are built, so they could be more easily converted into offices or apartments. Smart design and construction of new buildings would effectively future-proof them against obsolescence. Theoretically, an adaptable building could be repurposed continually for centuries.

Follow the Dream

At the beginning of this chapter, we compared smart cities to the fabulous cities of legend. We invited you to share our dream and to envision a world of smart cities and smart towns.

But smart cities aren't imaginary. They are not abstractions. They are real. In the months we spent researching and writing this book, we encountered naysayers and pessimists who told us that smart cities were a bad idea and an impossible dream. We disagree with the cynics.

Smart cities are gaining traction in every continent on the world. Legions of technology providers have already lined up to battle over shares in a market for smart-city solutions and services that's projected to exceed $1 trillion within the next five years.

The smart-city movement is part of a larger digital revolution. Digital technologies aren't simply transforming business and industry—they're transforming each and every aspect of our lives, including the places where we live. We are experiencing a genuine shift of paradigms; a new world is being born.

Like newborn infants, smart cities will experience growing pains. No two smart cities will be exactly alike. To varying degrees, smart cities will reflect the cultures and habits of the regions or nations in which they are located. Attempts to create one-size-fits-all models, cookie-cutter templates, or strict formulas for smart cities are unlikely to succeed. Smart cities will not be machines; they will grow and evolve, adapting like biological organisms to the changing environments around them.

Smart cities are not a panacea. They will not solve all the world's problems. Some will be more successful than others. Some will thrive and others will fail. There will be crime. There will be homelessness. There will be wealthy neighborhoods and poor neighborhoods.

But smart cities will engender hope. Their citizens will have a palpable sense of community. They will feel inspired and energized. They will be proud of their smart city. They will strive to keep it safe and clean. They will enjoy the wide variety of experiences and opportunities offered by the city. They will participate in governing their city and make their voices heard. They will be smart citizens.

We believe that cities have redemptive power. People choose to live in cities because they offer a social dynamism that's hard to find in small communities.

Cities are places where people can walk out their front doors and immediately begin having conversations with friends, neighbors, and even total strangers. They talk, they exchange ideas, and maybe they agree to start a business together. Or maybe they decide to have lunch, visit a museum, see a movie, or go for a walk down an avenue lined with shops.

Smart cities will offer the same opportunities, and more. A smart city will know when you're sick or injured and automatically dispatch emergency medics to help you. A smart city will turn on the lights when you enter a park at night – and turn them off when you leave. A smart city will remind you when it's time to renew your driver's license – and then help you renew it from your mobile phone. A smart city will help you find a good rehabilitation center if your mom slips and falls on the sidewalk.

In the chapters ahead, we describe smart-city projects of varying scale and complexity. We explain how smart cities are "systems of systems" and introduce key concepts, such as interoperability, open standards, resiliency, and continuous improvement. In addition to writing about smart cities, we share stories of smart towns, counties, regions, and nations.

We hope this book will become an indispensable resource as you engage more deeply with the smart-city movement and become more involved in planning our shared future.

As citizens, our roles in the development and evolution of smart cities will change continuously. One day we are observers, the next day we are active participants, adding our voices to the chorus. We hope you decide to play an active role and that the information in this book helps you become a smarter citizen in a world of smart cities.

Endnotes

1. Population Division of the Department of Economic and Social Affairs of the United Nations, *World Urbanization Prospects: The 2018 Revision* (New York: United Nations, 16 May 2018).

2. https://www.oreilly.com/iot/free/smart-cities-smarter-citizens.csp

3. https://esa.un.org/unpd/wup

4. http://davidalbouy.net/landvalue_index.pdf

5. http://countrymeters.info/en/Singapore

6. https://www.thesourcemagazine.org/peter-joo-hee-ng-chief-executive-pub-singapores-national-water-agency/

7. http://www.globalwaterforum.org/2018/01/15/newater-in-singapore/

8. https://www.pub.gov.sg/watersupply/singaporewaterstory

9. https://www.thesourcemagazine.org/peter-joo-hee-ng-chief-executive-pub-singapores-national-water-agency/

10. http://hdr.undp.org/en/content/what-human-development

11. https://visionzeronetwork.org/about/what-is-vision-zero

12. https://www.nfpa.org/-/media/Files/News-and-Research/Fire-statistics/Fact-sheets/SmokeAlarmsFactSheet.ashx?la=en

13. http://home-fire-risk.github.io/smoke_alarm_map

14. https://labs.enigma.com/smoke-signals

15. https://www.nfirs.fema.gov

16. http://www.datakind.org/blog/american-red-cross-and-datakind-team-up-to-prevent-home-fire-deaths-and-injuries

17. The phrase "a strong sense of a process unfolding" appears on page 13 of *Building and Dwelling* by Richard Sennett, in a reference to a description of Siena in an earlier book, *Architecture Without Architects*, by Bernard Rudofsky.

Chapter 2 ▬▬▬▬▬

Data Cities

JENNIFER ROBINSON is a long-serving member of the town council in Cary, North Carolina. Cary has a population of about 162,000 people and sits on the border of Research Triangle Park, one of the largest technology research parks in the world.[1]

Like most local governing bodies, the town council meets in the evening, and its nocturnal schedule allows Robinson to work a full-time day job at SAS, a large software company based in Cary. At SAS, her mission is bringing data science to local government.

"Traditionally, we focused on the federal and state levels," Robinson says. "Right now, data science is kind of optional at the municipal level. But I think it will be profoundly transformational. We're only at the beginning."

Robinson describes herself as "civically obsessed." She speaks with the passion of a true believer in the power of local government to make a positive difference in the lives of ordinary citizens. Robinson isn't alone in her beliefs. She represents a new generation of citizen-leaders who are genuinely comfortable with digital technologies and understand their potential as a force for good.

Her experiences have taught her that most citizens have faith in the basic principles of participatory democracy and good government. They also want their governments to serve them in ways that are meaningful, effective, efficient, and fair.

"What makes citizens happy? They need to feel safe," Robinson says. "They need to believe they have an equal chance to prosper. And they want to trust their government. When a government shares its data openly with citizens, it inspires trust. Open data enables citizens to explore and understand the actions and decisions of their government."

Citizens also know that knowledge and information translate into power. When governments have too much power, democracy is stifled. When people are kept in the dark or left out of decision-making processes, they disengage from civic life and the seeds of mistrust are sown. Open data, which can serve as a counterbalance to government power, has become a cornerstone of open democracy.[2]

Practical realities, rather than politics, are driving the open data movement. The mantra that "data is the new oil" has penetrated the culture. Citizens understand that data and information have real economic value. Unlike gold or silver, however, data is highly perishable. It's worthless if it's not being used. Locking it up in a vault destroys its value.

What is open data? "Open means anyone can freely access, use, modify, and share for any purpose (subject, at most, to requirements that preserve provenance and openness)," according to Open Definition,[3] a project of Open Knowledge International.[4]

Open data must be easily available and accessible (preferably via the Internet), machine readable, modifiable, reusable, and unrestricted.[5] In other words, open data can be downloaded and used by anyone for any purpose. By intention, it's fundamentally the opposite of proprietary data.

"When cities and towns put their data out there for public consumption, the data has a life of its own," says Robinson. She predicts open data will become "baseline" policy for municipal governments. "Open data has political support on both sides of the aisle. It's become a rallying point."

Open Is Smarter

Christina Franken leads the smart-cities program at Mapbox, an open-source location data platform used by web and mobile applications, such as Snapchat, Lonely Planet, Lyft, Weather.com, and Bloomberg News. Franken is also a strong advocate for open data.

"Open cities are smarter cities," she says. And she knows that there's more to sharing data than just posting it on public websites. She doubts the dream of smart cities can be realized without a combination of familiar technologies and open data. The good news is everybody knows how to use a smartphone. The bad news is that very few people know how to analyze data.

"Most citizens have no degree in data science, so merely publishing datasets on an open data portal won't be enough to make the open data really useful to everyone who can benefit from it," says Franken.

The remedy is fairly simple: Citizens and government workers should be trained to handle data. When people don't know how to use data, it doesn't matter whether it's open or closed.

"Open cities invest in transparent processes," she says. "They provide training and education, so everyone from government staffers to ordinary citizens can use the data."

Franken envisions a city "where all data is always open and accessible" and where "anybody, not only researchers and local activists" can access data and engage with it to prove a point." She foresees "transparency through open-by-default systems" in which trust is elevated and suspicions are reduced. "When all data is open and accessible, Big Brother–style creepiness is not possible," she says.

Part of becoming a smart city involves recognizing that many people will be frightened by, unaware of, or turned off by the terminology of data science. Cities will have to discover or invent easy ways for citizens to engage with data and use it productively. "Many new technologies seem scary at first, especially when there are lots of technical terms and buzzwords," says Franken. Smart cities that build on open data will help citizens overcome their suspicions, understand the potential benefits of data-driven processes, and get comfortable with the idea of treating some data as a commodity.

Not all data, of course, is open data. Personally identifiable information (PII) such as email addresses, names, and home addresses are not considered open data. Health care, financial, and many kinds of legal information are confidential and are not treated as open data. Fortunately, open data is usually more than sufficient for smart-city projects.

Holding hackathons and teaching young people how to write software using a local open dataset can greatly reduce the level of mystery around open data. After parents see their kids downloading a dataset of local air-quality data and writing a simple app with recommendations for those suffering from asthma, the whole idea of utilizing data to improve urban life becomes much more tangible.

Emma Mulqueeny is known in the software developer community for her efforts to popularize open data and teach programming skills to children. Young Rewired State (YRS), a charitable organization she founded in 2009, has taught thousands of children how to write software code and develop their own apps. She was recognized with an OBE—Officer of the Most Excellent Order of the British Empire—on Queen Elizabeth's 90th birthday honors list for services to technology and education.

Mulqueeny's stories and experiences reveal an emotional side of the smart-city narrative that is mostly overlooked. "When I first set up YRS, we used the same formula: gather open datasets, make sure they are clearly marked up, assemble young developers in a space, give them pizza, doughnuts, fruit and water, access to Wi-Fi, power, and mentors. Then let them be for 48 hours and see what they create," she recalls.

Over years of organizing YRS hackathons, she saw the emergence of consistent patterns. "Without fail, every time, in whichever country we were operating, around a third of the apps created by young people involved overlaying crime data on local maps and calculating the safest routes to school."

A cynical person might say, "Oh well, it's easy to create an app by laying crime data over a street map," but she saw it as the children expressing their need for safety. "Nobody told them to build an app for avoiding crime; they did it naturally."

Hacking in Berlin

Mulqueeny recalls a hackathon in Berlin at which the young programmers created maps from a database with the locations of all the gold plaques marking homes where Jewish people had lived before being taken away by the Nazis during World

War II. "The children created the maps, so visitors to the city could find the plaques more easily," she recalls.

The children also discovered "another database of Jewish people who had gone missing during the war and had no plaques because nobody knew where they had lived," Mulqueeny says. "The programmers created an interface enabling people to identify addresses against names and notify the city council, so new plaques could be laid for the missing people or their families."

She brought the same group of programmers to an EU conference in Lithuania, where they showcased the work they had done in Berlin. During the conference, they were approached by a woman from Kosovo who also was teaching young people to write software code.

"They had a list of 20,000 people who had gone missing in Kosovo and she asked our programmers to share the algorithm they had written for finding the lost people in Berlin," Mulqueeny explains. "Our group helped the Kosovar children create their own apps for identifying the homes of missing people in Kosovo. I love this story because it crosses borders, boundaries, and histories."

Mulqueeny also organized a hackathon in Kenya to reunite Somali refugees whose families had been split up when they crossed the border.

"There were plenty of workers on the ground to help reunite the families, but their tech was limited to mobile phones," she explains. "There were also problems matching people with their families, since many of the refugees had similar names or had lied about their names out of fear they would be harmed."

Since they couldn't rely on names, the programmers had to devise another strategy for identifying people who had been separated from their families and friends.

"Somalia has a rich storytelling culture," says Mulqueeny. So the programmers created a mobile app for recording stories from the refugees. "Then we wrote an algorithm for matching words and phrases in the stories. That's how we identified people who had come from the same village or the same family and reunited them."

Mulqueeny's stories vividly illustrate the many imaginative and innovative ways people can use data when it's easily available. "Data is only really useful when it's open," she says. "Data that's kept in closed accounts isn't all that helpful, especially when data needs to 'talk' freely across devices and networks."

Thousands of Layers

Today, many cities, counties, and states use data from geographic information systems (GISs) to create highly accurate three-dimensional maps showing the precise locations of critical infrastructure, such as roads, bridges, buildings, tunnels, natural gas lines, underground electric wiring, water mains, and sewer pipes.

"More than 15 percent of conventional addresses can be wrong, but 99 percent of properly geocoded addresses are right," says Alan Leidner, director of the Center for Geospatial Innovation of the Fund for the City of New York and president of the New York City Geospatial Information System and Mapping Organization (NYC GISMO).[6]

Not knowing the precise location of existing physical assets can delay construction projects (because workers aren't sure where it's safe for them to dig), impede disaster response and recovery efforts (because rescuers don't know where to look for survivors), and make planning for infrastructure development difficult (because cities are often built in layers and you need to know what's on the bottom before you build something on top of it).

Leidner was part of a team that mapped Ground Zero, the site of the World Trade Center towers, hours after they had been destroyed by al-Qaida terrorists flying hijacked passenger jets. Thick smoke, intense heat, twisted steel, and tons of fallen concrete made it difficult to pinpoint the location of underground infrastructure, including storage tanks containing 200,000 pounds of liquid Freon, which becomes toxic when vaporized.

"When the towers went down, the infrastructure 50 feet below them was damaged, too," Leidner explains. "So there were additional dangers, ranging from the potential collapse of the seawall on the Hudson River side, to underground fuel tanks that had caught fire."

The Freon tanks were hidden beneath the rubble, and nobody knew how close they were to the burning fuel tanks. "When you heat Freon, it turns into phosgene, a poison gas that was used during World War I," Leidner says. "You had hundreds of responders working down there, with fires burning all around them. We didn't want the Freon to vaporize and escape."

Using a combination of building plans and thermal imaging captured by helicopters, the mappers were able to determine the location of the Freon tanks in relation to the underground fires. The firefighters then doused the area between the tanks and the fires to prevent an additional catastrophe.

Today, the responders would have better access to precise maps showing the exact locations of every piece of infrastructure in the city, including underground tanks of potentially explosive chemicals.

"Most people think of GIS as a map. We see it as an integrator of hundreds of databases that would otherwise remain stuck in isolated silos," Leidner says. All of that data, he notes, can be analyzed and modeled for a wide range of useful purposes, from planning new parks and supporting work processes to predicting and responding to hurricanes.

In Australia, the city of Melbourne has created the Development Activity Model, a three-dimensional digital model showing building development and construction across the city. The model includes the locations of projects, construction details, and permit application numbers. A quick glance at the color-coded model will tell you whether a project is approved, waiting for approval, under construction, or completed.[7]

Melbourne's model is instructive and worth emulating; it makes it easier for all city stakeholders to keep track of development and construction. Melbourne has taken data visualization to a new level, and the results are impressive.

The Rise of Data Science

Ten years ago, the term "data science" typically evoked bewilderment, curiosity, and skepticism. There were breathless articles about the rise of data science. Suddenly it was cool to be a data scientist, even though no one was quite sure what the term meant. There were lively disagreements over who was a data scientist and who wasn't.

Then the world moved on and found other topics to argue about. Data science receded into the background, chugging along quietly beneath the radar, out of sight and out of mind. Slowly, it embedded itself into big business. Data scientists began showing up on the payrolls of investment banks, brokerage houses, and hedge funds. They spread to other parts of the commercial economy: travel, logistics, health care, pharmaceuticals, media, manufacturing, and retail.

Data science for government is a more recent phenomenon. Governments always drag their heels, arriving late for every party. But governments are catching up, and there are valid reasons for believing they will soon become leaders in data science.

Mike Holland is executive director of the Center for Urban Science and Progress (CUSP) at New York University. Local governments are adopting data science for practical purposes, he says.

"The demand for more high-quality public services is growing faster than available resources. As a result, public-sector agencies are facing relentless pressure to do more with less," Holland says. "Data science by itself is not a panacea, but good quality data and robust data science products can help agencies optimize operations, improve regulatory compliance, detect problems early, allocate scarce staff time, and drive evidence-based program management."

In addition to saving money, data science helps government become more open, more in touch, and more available. Instead of taking the bus or subway to city hall, you launch an app on your smartphone. Soon, the idea of standing on line at the motor vehicle department to renew your driver's license will seem positively medieval.

Ask any homeowner who's expanded a garage or remodeled a bathroom and they'll probably tell you the hardest part of the process was getting the construction permits from town hall. Waiting on line for the town zoning board and the building department to approve your new swimming pool or the spare bedroom you want to convert to a home office will be a thing of the past.

Data science offers more than convenience. It's also a methodology and a process for making sure that when you fill out an application, it doesn't get lost on someone's desk. Essentially, data science provides a framework for better government. Unless you're an anarchist, it's hard to argue against good government.

That said, there are legitimate concerns about the interplay between government and data science. In Shenzhen, China, a major city just north of Hong Kong, cameras linked to facial recognition systems post the names and faces of jaywalkers on large LED panels mounted above the intersection. It's a kind of public shaming that many societies would doubtless find objectionable. Shenzhen also plans to fine jaywalkers via text messaging, a step aimed at reducing the need to place LED panels large enough to show recognizable human faces at intersections across the city.[8]

Two large Chinese firms, SenseTime and Megvii, are pioneering combinations of facial recognition and artificial intelligence (AI) to create systems for spotting suspicious or unusual behavior in crowds and on street corners. Both firms sell products and services to government agencies.[9] Megvii says its Skynet system, which scans crowds for faces and crosschecks them with a criminal database, helped Chinese police agencies capture more than 3,000 fugitives nationwide in single year.[10]

Even if you're *not* a devotee of dystopian science fiction, you can imagine scenarios in which the marriage of data science and advanced surveillance technologies could have chilling effects.

It's important to acknowledge the dangers. It's also important not to fixate on them. All new technologies pose risks. There are downsides and unintended consequences. As a species, we are hardwired to overestimate our chances of success in every endeavor. We invariably fail more than we succeed. Our fundamental optimism isn't a weakness—it's the key to our survival.

In free societies, open data can mitigate the risk of governmental overreach. But people must feel empowered to become data users. Merely having data isn't enough—you need to know how to use it.

A Web of Information

"Local authorities sit in the middle of a web of information," writes Tom Symons, principal researcher for the Policy and Research team at Nesta,[11] a not-for-profit global innovation foundation based in the UK. "Everything from social care for vulnerable children, waste collection, procurement, council tax collection, to planning applications produces huge quantities of data."[12]

Quite a bit of that data is messy, unstructured, and difficult to manage. It arrives in large quantities and at high speeds from multiple sources. Buried in the data will be insights more valuable than rubies, emeralds, and diamonds. Good governments will dig out those insights and put them to work on behalf of their citizens.

"Running a city or a local authority is to a great extent about managing and responding to information," Symons writes. "And while big data presents opportunities for local councils, there are equally important opportunities presented by smaller datasets.... Whether the datasets are big or small, there are major benefits to be had from using them more intelligently, sharing them more widely, and making them more open."[13]

Saving Water and Protecting Children

For towns and cities, the benefits of sharing data range from reducing water usage to keeping children safer from abuse. Cary, North Carolina, for example, installed wireless water meters in 60,000 homes across the town. Reading meters manually once a month produced 12 data points per customer annually. The town's wireless system reads the meters hourly, creating 8,760 data points per customer annually.

The additional data points translate into usable knowledge. For instance, Cary can spot instances of unusual water usage, such as when someone leaves a garden hose running overnight or when a commercial dishwasher is malfunctioning. Town residents can use the system to track their own water usage. They can also sign up for alerts if the system detects unusual spikes in water consumption.

In the span of a typical year, the system collects roughly half a billion data points on water usage. The town uses the data to determine the scale and timing of new infrastructure projects, such as water plants, instead of relying on guesswork as it did in the past. With data science, Cary saved $10 million above the cost of upgrading its water meter system and expects to save more money in the future by analyzing its water usage scientifically, rather than haphazardly.[14]

State and local governments use data science to help citizens and their families in thousands of ways. In many states, local social services agencies use data science to reduce the chances of abused children being returned to abusive parents or guardians. "Caseworkers pull data from multiple systems, such as education, health care, criminal justice, and social services, to spot trends, identify key relationships, and reveal patterns that would be hidden to casual observers," Jennifer Robinson says.

Digging deep into the data enables caseworkers to keep more children out of potentially harmful situations. For example, when a prisoner is released, his or her address will be compared with the addresses in the town's child protective services system. If a match is found, an alert will be sent automatically to the caseworker responsible for the children at the address.

"Data science enables cities and counties to examine complex relationships between mental illness and rates of incarceration, see connections between childhood trauma and obesity, and discover underlying patterns in homelessness," Robinson says. Data analytics enable caseworkers to prioritize their cases, making it easier for them to focus on the children and families at the greatest risk.

Caseworkers are adopting the tools and processes of 21st-century data science to fulfill their roles as protective agents. Their new toolkits often include:

- Anomaly detection for uncovering abnormal patterns of behavior

- Predictive modeling for identifying new or emerging threats based on previous threats

- Network analysis for linking multiple parties through associative behavior or common ownership and identifying individuals associated with an at-risk child and capturing important data about them, such as criminal histories, behavioral health data, and drug or alcohol treatment data

- Adaptive segmentation with advanced neural networks

- Weighted scoring for each risk factor

- Automated monitoring and continuous recalculation of risk scores

- Alert engines to notify caseworkers when risk thresholds are exceeded

- Data visualization and reporting tools to share information quickly and easily.[15]

Supporting the efforts of data science–enabled caseworkers requires specialized software architectures and comprehensive data management systems. "No matter where the data is stored—whether it's in a legacy system or in a Hadoop data lake—you need the capabilities to access it," Robinson says. "You also need a hybrid approach to your analytics because you'll want to apply multiple techniques, such as anomaly detection, predictive modeling, social network analysis, and geospatial analysis."

Increasingly, cities and counties use advanced data science techniques, such as predictive modeling to reduce delinquency in child-support payments. "Predictive analytics allow caseworkers to identify situations that might result in delinquent payments," Robinson explains. "Having predictive capabilities allows caseworkers to distinguish between occasional lapses and systematic refusal to pay child support."

The idea of using data to solve social problems isn't new. What's new is enormous scale and scope of data, the widespread availability of practical tools for applying data science techniques outside of laboratories and classrooms, and the willingness of government workers to blend data science into their daily routines (Figure 2.1).

Cops, Firefighters, and Data Scientists

Every field has its own weird jargon. For data scientists, the term "large problem set" denotes a scenario in which the sheer size and complexity of the data overwhelms the capabilities of standard mathematics. Automated factories, self-driving taxis, long-range weather forecasting, global warfare simulations, piloting robot spacecraft through asteroid fields, next-day delivery of perishable drugs, and predicting the impact of climate change are examples of large problem spaces.

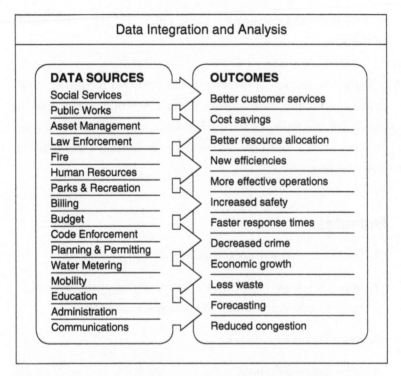

Figure 2.1 Smart communities collect, integrate, and analyze data to solve problems and help residents lead better lives. *Source: SAS.*

A large problem space defies both human intuition and traditional forms of statistical analysis. Specialized techniques of modern data science are required: artificial intelligence, machine learning, deep learning, natural language processing, and neural networks.

Smart cities are large problem spaces. In addition to police officers, firefighters, and sanitation workers, smart cities need data scientists. Within the next couple of years, no city will be able to function without data scientists. Small cities will have two or three data scientists; large cities will have thousands of them.

Data has become a valuable and important resource. Smart towns and cities will embrace data science and strive to maximize the value of their data. Data science will no longer be considered optional—it will be a fundamental part of how we live.

Endnotes

1. https://en.wikipedia.org/wiki/Research_Triangle_Park

2. https://www.sas.com/en_ca/insights/articles/analytics/local/open-source--open-data-and-open-government.html

3. https://opendefinition.org

4. https://okfn.org/about

5. https://opendefinition.org/od/2.1/en

6. http://www.gismonyc.org

7. https://developmentactivity.melbourne.vic.gov.au

8. https://motherboard.vice.com/en_us/article/wj7n74/china-jaywalking-facial-recognition-camera

9. https://www.npr.org/sections/parallels/2018/04/03/598012923/facial-recognition-in-china-is-big-business-as-local-governments-boost-surveilla

10. *Vice*, "A Face in the Crowd" episode, April 12, 2018.

11. https://www.nesta.org.uk/about-us

12. https://www.nesta.org.uk/blog/councils-and-data-revolution-7-ways-local-authorities-can-get-more-value-their-data

13. https://www.nesta.org.uk/blog/councils-and-data-revolution-7-ways-local-authorities-can-get-more-value-their-data

14. https://www.sas.com/en_us/customers/townofcary-aquastar.html

15. https://www.sas.com/en_us/software/analytics-for-child-well-being.html#sas-for-child-safety

Chapter 3

Cities in Motion

IF THE SCIENCE FICTION writers of the 1950s had been right, most of us today would travel around in flying cars and pneumatic trains. We would commute to work on high-speed moving sidewalks and zip across town in horizontal elevators. For short hops, we would wear personal jet packs or antigravity belts.

Well, here we are in the early 21st century and we're still waiting for buses, stuck in traffic jams, and trying to walk across busy streets without being hit by a cab. Transportation has changed, though not in the ways predicted by science fiction.

Many of the most important changes have been invisible. Today, cities routinely equip streets, roads, bridges, and tunnels with cameras and sensors. Traffic is monitored continuously, and many cities have installed adaptive systems for reprogramming traffic lights in real time to accommodate changes in traffic flows.

London, for example, uses the Split Cycle Offset Optimisation Technique, which monitors data from sensors and adjusts lights accordingly to keep traffic moving.[1] In Sydney, Australia, the Coordinated Adaptive Traffic System is used for similar purposes.[2]

The combination of millions of sensors, GPS, and advanced analytics has already revolutionized transportation and mobility, making it possible for cities to plan more intelligently for the future and to respond more quickly when problems or crises arise today.

Cities aren't the only interested parties in the global mobility revolution. Transportation is big business. In developed economies, transportation and logistics account for between 6 percent and 25 percent of GDP.[3] "The value of all transportation assets, including infrastructures and vehicles, can easily account for half the GDP of an advanced economy," writes Jean-Paul Rodrigue in *The Geography of Transport Systems*.[4]

As Rodrigue notes, "Efficient transportation reduces costs in many economic sectors, while inefficient transportation increases these costs." In cities, however, it's never easy to discern which kinds of transportation are efficient and which are not.

Constructing a new subway line might improve economic conditions in some areas and have adverse effects in other areas. Building a pedestrian walkway might make some parts of a neighborhood more accessible to foot traffic, yet store owners aren't likely to feel the benefits of the walkway unless it's used by their customers.

Additionally, the long time frames required for most transportation projects virtually guarantee changing conditions over the course of a project. A project that seems perfectly wonderful today might seem like a huge waste of time and money 10 years from now.

In the United States, the state of Texas spent $2.8 billion widening the Katy Freeway (Interstate 10) in Houston, long known for its terrible traffic jams. I-10 is now the world's widest freeway. Congestion eased for a while. Then it got worse and travel times increased as the widened freeway attracted more drivers.[5]

"When people are trying to solve an immediate problem, they often don't think about the ripple effects—the second-, third-, and fourth-degree consequences," says I-Ping Li, an innovation and analytics leader at Deloitte Consulting.

The ripple effects can be even more pronounced when new and disruptive technologies are involved. Cameras and sensors now allow cities to monitor traffic more closely than ever before. The ability to read license plate numbers of passing vehicles makes it relatively easy for cities to charge fees or levy fines on motorists driving through highly trafficked areas. It also makes it possible to offer speedier travel in express lanes for drivers willing to pay extra fees.[6]

Cities will be bombarded with plans and ideas from thousands of companies, organizations, agencies, groups, and institutions. City leaders will be forced to make hard choices, and many of them will find the allure of new technology irresistibly tempting.

Only a handful of the technology solutions they choose will produce the results that were expected. There will be unintended consequences, both good and bad. "It would be great if we all had better foresight," Li says.

Congestion Pricing

In 2003, London began charging motorists a hefty fee for driving their cars in the city's central area between 7 a.m. and 6 p.m. on weekdays. In addition to a daily fee (it's up to about $16 now), there are steep charges for late payments.

The program worked, but not as expected. Many people stopped driving their private cars into the city center. And for a while, traffic improved. But then it got worse.

What happened? The private cars were replaced by private-hire vehicles and ridesharing services such as Uber. For a while, congestion got so bad that Londoners began avoiding buses. On the other hand, the congestion prompted more Londoners to ride bicycles to work, which in turn created a need for more bike lanes.

London's congestion pricing program wasn't a failure; it substantially reduced the number of private cars in the city center and forced Londoners to rethink how they use transportation. London's program has been widely studied, and other large cities, including Stockholm, Singapore, and Milan, have adopted their own versions. A plan to bring congestion pricing to New York City fell victim to state-level politics, although advocates are still hoping to revive it.[7]

But London's experience with congestion pricing reveals the inherent difficulties of mounting large-scale smart-city projects. It also shows the value of sticking with a program, even when the results and benefits are uncertain.

Smart-city projects are rarely one-and-done affairs; they require continual testing, refinement, and improvement. Eventually London will get its congestion pricing right, and the world will benefit from the city's experiment.

Expanding Opportunities

Within a relatively brief span of time, ridesharing services, such as Uber and Lyft, have dramatically transformed urban mobility. The distribution of benefits, however, has been uneven. In affluent areas, for example, ridesharing may reduce traffic congestion. In less affluent areas and in commercial zones, however, ridesharing can add to congestion.

Here's why: in affluent areas, people use ridesharing as an alternative form of transportation. In other words, when they use ridesharing, they leave their cars at home.

In less affluent areas, where public transit services are stretched thin and taxicabs are often scarce, ridesharing quickly becomes an economic necessity. In poorer neighborhoods, ridesharing fills the gaps left by traditional forms of transportation and creates new opportunities for commuting to jobs in other parts of the city.

Moreover, ridesharing penetrates areas of the city that traditional cabs and livery services tend to avoid. In some cities, ridesharing transforms marginal areas into commutable neighborhoods, opening up opportunities for workers and rejuvenating local economies.

"We see ourselves as a partner to public transit," says Joseph Okpaku, vice president of government relations at Lyft. "Many Lyft passengers integrate rideshare trips with public transit as part of their regular commute."

More than a third of Lyft rides in New York City start or end near a transit station, Okpaku says. "Twenty-three percent of weekend rides in New York happen between midnight and 5 a.m.," he says. "And 40 percent of Lyft rides take place in the city's outer boroughs," which have higher concentrations of poor neighborhoods than other parts of New York.

The company has entered into direct partnerships with some municipalities, Okpaku says. "For example, we are partnering with San Clemente and the Orange County Transportation Authority to help ensure uninterrupted transportation access for San Clemente residents after two bus routes went out of service."

The partnership, he says, demonstrates how an "on-demand ridesharing service offers convenience and efficiency in a low-density suburban area, where it's difficult to operate frequent, fixed-route service."

In the *CityLab* article "Lyft Is Reaching L.A. Neighborhoods Where Taxis Wouldn't," Laura Bliss generally supports Okpaku's contention that ridesharing can help disadvantaged communities and create more economic opportunities in poor neighborhoods.[8] While Bliss carefully avoids taking sides in the article, it seems clear that ridesharing is having a positive impact in Los Angeles.

Citing a groundbreaking dissertation by Anne Elizabeth Brown from UCLA's Institute for Transportation Studies,[9] Bliss writes, "Virtually no neighborhood in the country's most densely populated urban area[10] has been left unpenetrated by Lyft. The company's drivers serve 99.8 percent of the population of L.A. County. That in itself suggests that communities aren't being systematically excluded."

Ridesharing also offers time and cost efficiencies. A 2017 study by INRIX[11] showed that drivers spend an average of 17 hours a year searching for parking spots. Ridesharing allows people to spend more time at their intended destinations—and less time on aimless driving.

"We believe people can lead fuller, more productive lives by reducing their reliance on personal vehicles," Okpaku says.

"Throughout much of the 20th century to now, we've built our communities entirely around cars. And for the most part, we've built them for cars that aren't even moving."

The average vehicle is used only 4 percent of the time and is parked the other 96 percent, he says. "Parked cars reduce capacity of our streets and roadways—space which instead could be redesigned around people and bringing communities together," he says.

Car Culture Remains Strong

It's logical for ridesharing services, such as Lyft and Uber, to evangelize for reductions in personal car ownership and to promote their ability to provide first mile/last mile transportation. The era of personal vehicles, however, is far from over.

In the US, for example, there is still predominately a car culture. The vast majority of commuters in the United States drive to their jobs. Only 5 percent of US commuters use transit. That simple fact helps explains why US cities have a hard time getting public funds for transit.[12]

It also partly explains why autonomous vehicles (AVs) haven't gained wider popularity. Numerous surveys have shown that people don't want to stop driving—even when it's inconvenient, expensive, and dangerous. Rather than sitting as passengers in AVs, people want cars that are easier to drive and easier to park.[13]

For most people, autonomy is a fuzzy concept. Autonomy has multiple levels, adding to the confusion. In the United States, the Federal Automated Vehicles Policy[14] relies on a multilevel definition of autonomy created by SAE International,[15] a mobility engineering standards organization. Here are the levels, as defined by SAE:

Level 0—The human driver does everything.

Level 1—An automated system on the vehicle can sometimes assist the human driver conduct some parts of the driving task.

Level 2—An automated system on the vehicle can actually conduct some parts of the driving task, while the human continues to monitor the driving environment and performs the rest of the driving task.

Level 3—An automated system can both actually conduct some parts of the driving task and monitor the driving environment in some instances, but the human driver must be ready to take back control when the automated system requests.

Level 4—An automated system can conduct the driving task and monitor the driving environment, and the human need not take back control, but the automated system can operate only in certain environments and under certain conditions.

Level 5—The automated system can perform all driving tasks under all conditions that a human driver could perform.

Will the Car Find a Parking Spot?

A 2017 study of nearly 3,000 people by the Massachusetts Institute of Technology AgeLab[16] and the New England Motor Press Association reveals a rising level of antipathy towards the concept of fully autonomous driving. "Nearly half of respondents indicated they would never purchase a car that completely drives itself," according to study.

When asked to explain why they would never buy an autonomous car, most respondents indicated that would be uncomfortable with the loss of control. "Other commonly mentioned factors included not trusting the technology, a disbelief that it would be robust enough to rely on exclusively, and a feeling that self-driving cars are unsafe."[17]

The World Economic Forum (WEF), in collaboration with the Boston Consulting Group, recently studied the potential impact of AVs on Boston. According to the study, "AVs enable the greatest transformation in urban mobility since the creation of the automobile." The study also shows that consumers are mainly "interested in avoiding traffic jams and being productive in the car...the single most important benefit of AVs is not having to look for parking."[18]

Consumers interviewed for the study said they want cars that will perform three essential tasks:

1. Drop off the driver, find a parking spot, and park on its own.

2. Allow drivers to multitask and be productive during rides.

3. Switch to self-driving mode in traffic.[19]

Many carmakers have already built varying degrees of autonomy into their vehicles, although no manufacturer offers a fully operational autonomous vehicle that's ready to drive itself out of the showroom and park itself in your garage while you nap in the back seat.

Learning to Love Big Data

Despite wavering consumer interest, we believe automotive technology will eventually improve to the point where autonomous self-driving vehicles become the norm. For cities, however, the big unanswered question is whether those AVs will make life better or worse.

It's easy to imagine scenarios in which downtown areas are choked with self-driving cars during the morning rush hour. It's also easy to imagine those cars conveniently parking themselves after dropping off their occupants. That said, where will they park themselves? Will the post–rush hour become a muddle of automated cars jostling to find parking spots?

Some of these questions may be answered by data science. A typical car generates 25 gigabytes of data per hour and 130 terabytes per year. A fully autonomous car would probably generate 80 terabytes of data in a single day. The data produced by cars and other vehicles will be used to feed analytic models that will help software developers and engineers build the next generation of smart-city transportation systems.

"Mobility has become a big data problem," says Vijay Raja, solutions marketing lead for IoT at Cloudera, an early pioneer in the open-source data analytics and machine learning space. "All of these vehicles are equipped with thousands of sensors and they generate enormous amounts of data. Pretty soon, the data from cars will be worth more than the cars themselves."

Dave Shuman, an IoT and manufacturing industry leader at Cloudera, agrees that data is the key to solving many of the transportation challenges facing smart cities. Cities are just beginning to develop the capabilities they'll need for collecting and sorting through the data required to make intelligent decisions about mobility.

That data will come from many sources. In addition to analyzing data from vehicles and video cameras, cities will need to analyze data from sensors in streets, buildings, sidewalks, lampposts, utility poles, storage tanks, storm drains, sewer covers, and aerial drones. Cities will also want to monitor data exchanged between vehicles and data exchanged between vehicles and infrastructure, adding multiple layers of complexity to the problem.

"Cities will mix and combine vast amounts of data, as well as providing context to make the data usable," Shuman says. Many cities and states are beginning to develop expertise in machine learning and other types of advanced data analysis that reveal underlying patterns in traffic and automatically spot the difference between normal and abnormal situations.

The Kentucky Transportation Cabinet, for example, aggregates 15–20 million records per day and processes more than a million records per second to optimize its responses to adverse road conditions in bad weather. The state incorporates sensor data from its fleet of snowplows and trucks, and combines it with real-time traffic and weather data from a variety of third-party sources, including Waze, Esri, and HERE, to plan snow-plowing and salt-spreading routes, and to predict how much material they will use, potentially saving the state millions of dollars in costs every year.

The school system in Saratoga Springs, New York, uses a predictive maintenance solution from Navistar to monitor the condition of school buses in real time, greatly reducing unexpected breakdowns and virtually eliminating the need for emergency towing. Municipalities are also using combinations of telematics and big-data analytics to lower insurance premiums.[20]

Multimodal Mobility

Smart cities will also use big data to optimize multimodal commuting. Let's say you drive your car to a downtown parking garage, and your office is another 10 blocks away. If the weather is nice, you might consider walking or perhaps using a bikeshare service. If it's raining or snowing, you'll want to know the location of the nearest bus stop and when the next bus is scheduled to arrive. Or you might simply prefer to hail a cab or summon a ridesharing car.

There are plenty of smart-phone apps that will give you walking directions, guide you to a metro station, or tell you when the next train is arriving. Yet there are relatively few apps that will help you combine different modes of travel. Meeting of the Minds recently published a useful list of innovative urban transit apps,[21] but even those apps won't provide you with seamless intermodal connections.

The WEF predicts that commuters of the future will use integrated proactive intermodal travel assistants (IPITAs) to figure out the best combinations of travel options.[22] IPITAs, says the WEF, will "optimize intermodal travel planning, booking, and navigation, using real-time maps and geospecific information." They will link to traffic management systems for multiple modes (e.g., road, rail, and air) and will send real-time alerts when travel disruptions occur. The WEF foresees IPITAs providing "a single, seamless interface that includes one mobile ticket across all modes of travel."

Boyd Cohen, a smart-city entrepreneur, wants to take the concept of seamless intermodal travel a step further, proposing a blockchain-based token that will serve as currency in cities with smart mobility systems.

Cohen is a founder and CEO of IoMob, a firm whose goal is "empowering local mobility entrepreneurs[23] to compete on an even playing field with multinational mobility companies while enabling seamless access to intermodal public and private transit solutions."[24] He envisions building an Internet of Mobility that would serve as a platform for new services based on mobility-as-a-service models.

"IoMob, for example, aims to decentralize urban mobility through an Internet of Mobility (IoM) protocol," he writes.[25] For example, an individual taxi driver would "tap into an app and plug into an open blockchain protocol and be discoverable by an open network of mobility users."

IoMob is a founding member of the newly formed Blockchain Cities Alliance,[26] an organization of groups dedicated to expanding the use of decentralized blockchain applications in smart cities. The alliance represents a convergence of blockchain and smart-city technologies developed through collaborative processes. In that respect, it is the face of a new generation of smart-city entrepreneurs and activists.

Battling Complacency

In *A Tale of Two Cities*, Charles Dickens includes a heartbreaking scene in which a Parisian child is struck and killed by a speeding carriage. The carriage's owner, a powerful nobleman, tosses a gold coin toward the child's grieving father, after berating the city dwellers who have gathered and blaming the fatal accident on their carelessness.

We've come a long way since then – or at least we like to think we have. Today, conversations about transportation often focus on new ways for alleviating traffic congestion, providing more travel options for commuters, and making it easier for drivers to find parking spaces.

What's often missing from the conversations, however, is the issue of safety. We all dread being stuck in traffic jams. But it's far worse being involved in a traffic crash. "Mobility is a very human-centered problem," says Leah Shahum, founder and director of the Vision Zero Network, a nonprofit organization dedicated to eliminating deaths and injuries from traffic crashes.[27]

"Traffic crashes kill 40,000 people annually in the U.S. and injure millions more. We can do more to prevent this suffering and we believe all of us — whether we're driving, walking, bicycling, using a wheelchair, or riding transit — have a basic right to safe mobility," Shahum says.

Traditional solutions often fail to address basic safety issues, such as maintaining physical separation between those walking, bicycling, driving, and taking transit. Some forward-thinking communities are building "complete streets," which are streets designed to separate traffic and reduce the chances and severity of collisions.[28]

There are many alternatives to the status quo that don't require high-tech solutions or major capital investments. One of the most effective ways to prevent serious traffic crashes is by managing speeds, especially on streets used by those walking and bicycling.

Fatalism, acceptance, and complacency are some of the biggest obstacles to achieving higher levels of safety, Shahum says. "It reminds me of the early days of the anti-smoking movement. Back then, most people thought there was nothing anybody could do to curtail smoking, but look how far we've come in such a relatively short time."

As a civil society, she says, there's no reason to be complacent about thousands of traffic deaths every year. "Almost all those deaths are avoidable. New York City adopted a Vision Zero program four years ago and they've reduced traffic deaths by 28 percent.[29] In Sweden, where the program began 20 years ago, they've cut traffic deaths in half."[30]

Shahum says she's seeing the beginnings of a slow and steady cultural shift. In the future, people will look back at our time and wonder why we didn't act sooner to prevent traffic deaths, she says.

"We're not talking about restricting mobility," Shahum says. "We all want to be as mobile as possible. At the same time, everyone relates to safety because everyone knows someone who's been in a serious traffic crash. If we take a systematic approach, we can have both safety and mobility."

Moving Goods and People

Solving mobility challenges requires finding an appropriate balance among multiple factors, such as cost, speed, efficiency, safety, and quality of life. Miscalculating or mis-judging any of those variables can doom a project, wasting years of time and astronomical sums of money.

"Cities and states take a long-term view when they plan transportation infrastructure. Nothing is going to happen overnight," says Kirk Steudle, director of the Michigan Department of Transportation. Steudle oversees the department's $4.7 billion annual budget and is responsible for the construction, maintenance, and operation of nearly 10,000 miles of state highways and more than 4,000 state highway bridges. He also oversees a wide range of multimodal transportation programs statewide.[31]

Steudle is understandably wary of large-scale projects that depend heavily on pouring concrete and bending steel. He feels inspired, however, by a local initiative providing autonomous electric shuttle bus service in Detroit, a city that was the heart and soul of the automotive industry for decades. The self-driving shuttle service is a partnership between May Mobility, an Ann Arbor start-up, and Bedrock, a real estate firm in downtown Detroit, an area that has become a hub for technology firms.

The six-seat electric shuttles have become a familiar sight within a one-mile loop in the downtown area. They blend easily into the traffic flow, moving quietly among cars, cyclists, and pedestrians. "I rode in a shuttle and it absolutely responds to pedestrians the same way you would expect a driver to respond," Steudle says. "This isn't a test—it's a real service with actual passengers."

The success of the Detroit initiative would seem to bode well for the concept of small-scale self-driving transit services for short-distance travel. Similar projects in other cities have failed, however, mostly because they attracted few riders. Detroit's microtransit system targets a specific audience of potential riders who work in the downtown area, but there are no guarantees they will remain loyal to the shuttle service after the novelty wears off.

Steudle warns against becoming overly enamored of any one particular scenario, even when the numbers are impressive. Statistics can be misleading, especially when they focus on a small group of metrics. For example, vehicle miles traveled (VMT) is a measure commonly used by the Federal Highway Administration. VMT metrics are highly fluid and can be swayed by many variables, such as fuel prices, weather, demographics, and changing lifestyles.[32]

"Some studies predict lower VMTs because people will be sharing cars, but other studies show VMTs quadrupling because we'll have all of these empty cars driving around," Steudle says.

Jobs and Access to Transit

Given the high levels of uncertainty and unpredictability, why should cities go to the trouble of solving transportation and mobility problems for residents and commuters?

The standard argument is that transportation is a public good and provides manifold benefits to society that cannot

be readily measured. In an era of tight budgets and linger-
ing mistrust of central governments, simply labeling something a public good isn't enough to win votes from skeptical
taxpayers.

Another argument is that transportation is a keystone
issue—cities that solve their transportation problems will find
it easier to cope with other pressing urban challenges, such
as energy efficiency, public safety, environmental protection,
waste management, and economic inequality.

A detailed study[33] published in 2018 by the Accessibility Observatory, a program of the Center for Transportation
Studies at the University of Minnesota, ranks the cities in
the United States with the best access to transit. "The top
cities should be no surprise: New York, San Francisco, and
Chicago all have a combination of dense downtowns and
high-speed trains that can transport workers from suburbs.
Other high-ranking cities, like Seattle and Denver, rely more
on frequent bus networks and expanding light rail service,
showing there's no one-size-fits-all approach," writes Jason
Plautz in Smart Cities Dive.[34]

The study also points to a connection between a city's
economic health and its ability to provide access to jobs by
transit. Common sense tells us there's a relationship between
jobs and transit, yet the precise nature of the relationship
is difficult to measure objectively and will likely remain
a conundrum.

The Bottleneck at Morrill's Corner

In Portland, Maine, five roads intersect at a spot called Morrill's Corner. The result is a daily traffic jam of epic proportions. The city has embarked on a project to reduce the gridlock, using a system of radar sensors and real-time traffic signals devised in the Robotics Institute at Carnegie Mellon University.[35]

The system is called Surtrac, and if it works, Portland hopes to extend its use to other parts of the city where traffic is a problem. Evaluating and fine-tuning the system will take time.

"We're at the very beginning stages of implementation," explains Portland City Manager Jon Jennings. Because the system uses artificial intelligence, it will take time for it to "learn" the nuances and peculiarities of the local traffic patterns. Jennings is optimistic and sees value in the experiment. "I am very pleased with the fact that we took the leadership and installed the first integrated traffic signals in the entire state. I do believe they will work."

Portland is a small city and it takes pride in its long history as a seaport. It's a city of neighborhoods with names such as Cushing's Island, Stroudwater, Rosemont, Nason's Corner, Lunt's Corner, and Morrill's Corner.

Mainers appreciate new technology. They also enjoy a sense of being detached from popular trends and passing fads. They're reserving judgment on the new system for relieving the bottleneck at Morrill's Corner.

They're aware of being pioneers in a new form of civic engagement. If the system is successful, it will do more than merely reduce traffic tie-ups. It will lower carbon emissions, contribute to cleaner air, and make the city more livable. It will help Portland, which is one of Maine's primary destinations for tourism, maintain its image as a vintage New England community.

It will also encourage other cities and towns to experiment with similar projects. In that sense, it's a small but significant step forward in a long a complicated journey.

Transportation and mobility issues are inherently complex and hard to solve. They are also highly visible, which means they cannot be easily dismissed. When people visit a city, their first impressions are strongly influenced by the quality of their interactions with its transportation systems. Smart cities will spend the time and money necessary to make certain those first impressions are favorable.

Endnotes

1. https://trlsoftware.co.uk/products/traffic_control/scoot

2. http://www.scats.com.au

3. https://transportgeography.org/?page_id=5260

4. https://transportgeography.org

5. http://cityobservatory.org/reducing-congestion-katy-didnt

6. https://www.wsdot.wa.gov/Tolling/405/default.htm

7. https://www.nytimes.com/2018/03/31/nyregion/congestion-pricing-new-york.html

8. https://www.citylab.com/transportation/2018/06/lyft-is-reaching-la-neighborhoods-where-taxis-wouldnt/563810

9. https://escholarship.org/uc/item/4r22m57k

10. https://la.curbed.com/2012/3/26/10385086/los-angeles-is-the-most-densely-populated-urban-area-in-the-us

11. http://inrix.com/press-releases/parking-pain-us

12. https://www.brookings.edu/blog/the-avenue/2017/10/03/americans-commuting-choices-5-major-takeaways-from-2016-census-data

13. http://www.wbur.org/bostonomix/2017/05/25/mit-study-self-driving-cars

14. https://www.transportation.gov/AV/federal-automated-vehicles-policy-september-2016

15. https://www.sae.org

16. http://agelab.mit.edu/about-agelab

17. http://agelab.mit.edu/sites/default/files/MIT%20-%20NEMPA%20White%20Paper%20FINAL.pdf

18. http://www3.weforum.org/docs/WEF_Reshaping_Urban_Mobility_with_Autonomous_Vehicles_2018.pdf

19. ibid

20. https://www.cloudera.com/more/customers/octo-telematics
    .html

21. http://meetingoftheminds.org/12-innovative-urban-
    transportation-apps-4708

22. http://reports.weforum.org/connected-world-2013/ipita-
    integrated-proactive-intermodal-travel-assistant

23. https://medium.com/iomob/empowering-taxi-drivers-in-a-
    fully-decentralized-internet-of-mobility-out-uber-uber-
    7beaf5f40b6c

24. https://medium.com/iomob/announcing-the-launch-of-the-
    blockchain-cities-alliance-79b4291450f4

25. https://medium.com/iomob/why-smart-cities-must-embrace-
    decentralization-the-case-for-blockchain-cities-d52231e89892

26. http://blockchaincities.io

27. https://visionzeronetwork.org/

28. https://smartgrowthamerica.org/program/national-complete-
    streets-coalition/

29. https://www1.nyc.gov/office-of-the-mayor/news/016-18/
    vision-zero-mayor-de-blasio-pedestrian-fatalities-dropped-32-
    last-year-making-2017#/0

30. https://www.weforum.org/agenda/2018/04/sweden-zero-
    vision-traffic-road-deaths/

31. https://www.michigan.gov/mdot/0,4616,7-151-9623_10724-
    61418--,00.html

32. https://www.advisorperspectives.com/dshort/updates/2018/
07/02/vehicle-miles-traveled-another-look-at-our-evolving-
behavior

33. http://www.cts.umn.edu/Publications/ResearchReports/
reportdetail.html?id=2694

34. https://www.smartcitiesdive.com/news/new-york-city-job-
access-via-transit/527002

35. http://www.surtrac.net

Chapter 4

Forces of Attraction

"SMART CITIES are cities that learn," says Jerry MacArthur Hultin, chairman of the Global Futures Group, an advisory firm that helps cities, states, nations, and companies develop and manage smart-city projects. "They learn by collecting and analyzing data generated by the city's buildings, streets, machines, and people. They use that data to help people thrive and to improve the quality of life."

Smart cities put people first, Hultin says. They adapt and evolve to meet the changing needs of the people who depend on them for shelter, safety, work, food, education, and entertainment. They provide a sense of belonging and acceptance.

Smart cities seek to shape and control their own destinies, Hultin says. They compete with other cities by attracting talent. Smart cities are more than collections of smart machines, smart data networks, smart power grids, and smart transportation systems—they're magnets for smart people.

Cities of the future will pursue many of the same economic development strategies pursued by cities today. In addition to competing for big-name companies and major league sports teams, however, they will compete for the best and brightest citizens. Civic pride and bragging rights will play roles in the competition for smart citizens, but the fundamental motivating force will be economic survival. Smart cities will need smart people to drive their economies. They'll need them to launch new businesses, invent new technologies, discover cures for diseases, and design beautiful buildings. Smart people are the true capital of smart cities.

"A truly innovative and self-sustaining city will need lots of bright people doing bright things," he says. "The city will need smart infrastructure and technology assets to attract and retain the best people. Cities that aren't smart will slowly fall behind. Eventually they will disappear."

Racing to Quality

Competitions, such as the US Department of Transportation's Smart City Challenge, UC Berkeley's Global Social Venture Competition, the IEEE's Smart Cities Mega Challenge, Canada's Smart Cities Challenge, and NextChallenge: Smart Cities, contribute to the smart-city evolutionary process by providing impetus, motivation, recognition—and in some instances, substantial cash awards. They also become focal points for peer-to-peer networking and knowledge sharing.

Amazon's highly publicized search for the site of its second headquarters (#HQ2) also moved the ball forward by encouraging cities to take inventory of their smart-city capabilities and to update the metrics they use for assessing their progress compared with other cities. The Smart Cities Mission launched by India's Ministry of Urban Development in 2015 is having a similarly beneficial impact by pushing cities to examine their unique resources from 21st-century perspectives and to reconsider how they will measure success in the future.

The competitions served a useful purpose by galvanizing efforts and providing common ground for people with similar passions and goals. It would be easy to criticize smart-city competitions or to dismiss them as a form of ordinary hucksterism,[1] but it's important to remember that almost every major global industry (e.g., aerospace, automotive, information technology, media, and entertainment) has a long tradition of holding contests and competitions. The winners gain recognition and awards, and all the cities that compete benefit from the intensive analysis and self-assessment they carried out as they prepared their bids.

Interest in the smart cities movement has also spawned hundreds of conferences, expos, summits, seminars, and symposia. The contests and events add momentum, create a sense of urgency, and draw attention to the movement.

Merited or unmerited, the attention has a positive effect. Cities are beginning to analyze their strengths and weaknesses more carefully and at levels that are more granular. They're using new criteria to grade themselves and are asking themselves questions that are more relevant to modern citizens and consumers of services.

Cities are no longer defining success in purely economic terms; the calculus has become more nuanced and refined. Cities are looking at themselves and asking new combinations of questions:

- Are we energy efficient?

- Are we resilient?

- Are we ready to handle a broad spectrum of threats and challenges, ranging from storms, floods, and fires to cybercrime, terrorism, pandemics, and the rise of robots?

- Are we adaptable, flexible, and agile?

- Do the people we serve feel happy, healthy, secure, and satisfied with their lives?

Cities are raising the bar and upping their games. Why now? What's really driving the smart-city movement? There are thousands of factors influencing, propelling, and energizing the smart-city movement. From our perspective, the three primary drivers of change are:

1. Hypercompetitive global markets

2. Rapidly diminishing resources

3. Shifting expectations from a rising generation of digital natives

"We're seeing a race to quality," Hultin says. "Cities are thinking seriously about how they can become smarter, cleaner, safer, and more livable. They're thinking energy efficiency, sustainability, and resiliency. And they're wondering how they measure up against other cities in the competition to attract and retain the smartest and most talented people."

Punching a Featherbed

Hultin isn't a misty-eyed visionary. After serving in the US Navy and seeing action in the Vietnam War, he returned to civilian life and graduated from Yale Law School. Bill and Hillary Clinton were classmates. They remained friends over the next two decades, and in 1997, President Clinton tapped him for the role of Under Secretary of the Navy, the second-highest ranking civilian official in the US Department of the Navy.

Hultin's signature effort at the Department of the Navy was the consolidation of information technology services and the creation of a single intranet for the Navy and the Marine Corps. The scope and magnitude of the problem presented enormous challenges.

"The Navy is a big enterprise. We had about 800,000 people. We had 400 wide area networks. Each network had its own administrator and its own applications. We were supporting roughly 100,000 applications," Hultin recalls.

Communications between networks was difficult. "One network would be running Excel, another network would be running Lotus 123. It was difficult updating the applications and keeping people trained," he says.

The Navy put out bids and contracted with a private vendor, EDS, to untangle the mess and create a unified intranet. Hultin invokes the words of Franklin Delano Roosevelt, who served as Assistant Secretary of the Navy from 1913 until 1920, to convey the nature of the challenge:

> *To change anything in the Na-a-vy is like punching a feather bed. You punch it with your right and you punch it with your left until you are finally exhausted, and then you find the damn bed just as it was before you started punching.*

With all due respect to FDR, he didn't anticipate Hultin's tenacity. The Navy Marine Corps Intranet (NMCI) project was completed and became a model for the armed forces. The consolidation and modernization effort had an unanticipated benefit: It added resiliency to the Navy's infotech capabilities. That resiliency, says Hultin, enabled the Navy's information systems to recover much more quickly than the systems operated by the other military branches after the attack on the Pentagon on Sept. 11, 2001

A Billion Saved Is a Billion Earned

Hultin's first-hand experience managing large, sprawling, multidimensional programs, such as the NMCI, gives him a unique perspective into the challenges and opportunities confronting smart cities.

"For example, the Pentagon spends about $200 billion on back-office operations, such as human resources, finance, logistics, and facilities. Applying AI and automation to some of those processes could reduce operating costs by 30 percent and speed decision- making by 100 times," Hultin says. "Imagine if we applied some of those ideas here in New York City, which has an annual budget of roughly $85 billion.[2] We might save $25 billion. Instead of spending tax dollars on back-office operations, we could invest the money in housing, education, and mental health. That's how a smart city works."

The idea that money saved through cost reductions can and should be reinvested in citizen services isn't new. What's different now is the potential scale of the savings that will be achieved by using AI and automation to reduce headcount, cut red tape, and streamline bureaucratic processes.

Even if technology doesn't erase job categories, it will replace many of the common tasks that make up a typical day's work. As a result, it will take less time—and fewer people—to get work done. City bureaucracies that once required hundreds of workers will require only dozens. And the workers will provide answers and approvals in minutes and hours, not days and weeks.

Smart cities will save money by scaling back or eliminating jobs involving tedious, repetitive tasks. Ideally, the unspent money will be reallocated to hire people for high-skill, high-touch jobs that cannot be performed by machines, such as teaching, nursing, counseling, policing, and the entirely new job categories that will arise as smart-city economies evolve and mature.

It's also possible that smart cities will create enough new jobs to make up for many of the jobs lost through automation. A significant fraction of those new jobs will require advanced skills, such as the ability to code software, analyze spreadsheets, think creatively, interact effectively with complex information systems, work independently, and, when necessary, collaborate meaningfully with teams of colleagues in nontraditional or virtual spaces.

Workers with the critical skills sought by employers will be well compensated. But what will happen to the millions of workers who, for various reasons, cannot be retrained and reabsorbed into modern complex economies? How will they survive, succeed, and find happiness in smart cities?

To be fair, private-sector jobs far outnumber public-sector jobs in most cities, so thinning the ranks of municipal workers wouldn't result in massive unemployment or widespread economic dislocations. Yet it would be painful for the individuals whose jobs are eliminated and for their families.

What will smart cities do to counter the negative impacts of lost jobs? There are no easy answers or entirely palatable solutions. It seems clear that K–12 schools will need to update their curricula and include computer science as a requisite skill for all students. Cities themselves will have to become much better at providing free or affordable modularized certificate-based technical training for citizens who want or need to change careers.

Cities may have to provide free or affordable health care for more citizens, because most people lose their health care insurance when they lose their jobs. The smartest cities will promote and enable PPPs and innovative cooperatives that will offer education and preventive care to help people stay healthy.

Big Brother and the Nanny State

There are legitimate concerns that smart cities could easily become Orwellian dystopias. Becoming a smart city means using many of the same tools and techniques that would be used by a modern totalitarian state. You can't be a smart city without deploying millions of sensors and thousands of cameras, all connected through networks and feeding information into real-time analytics.

Some societies are already pairing facial recognition technology with advanced database tools to sniff out nascent political movements and crack down on social activists.

Even the most benign smart cities will have to endure criticism that they are evolving into nanny states, because to some degree they'll have no other choice but to become more protective of their citizens. People who are out of work or constantly worried about losing their jobs often become anxious and depressed. Untreated anxiety and depression can destroy lives and families. For some people, untreated chronic psychological problems can lead to a broad range of destructive behaviors, including drug abuse, alcoholism, and violence.

Smart cities will anticipate the problems facing their citizens and develop programs to help citizens deal with their personal issues before they metamorphose into public safety threats.

Cities that aspire to becoming smarter will also begin debating the issues that are bound to arise as continuous surveillance becomes the norm. Now is the time for cities to form committees, panels, and working groups whose members will begin the long process of developing new guidelines, rules, and regulations that will prevent smart cities from becoming omniscient Peeping Toms.

Flatter Organizations and Circular Economies

Smart cities will use technology, data science, and 21st-century governance principles to help people live better, healthier, and happier lives—that's the dream. Turning those visions into concrete reality will be a job for everyone. It cannot be a top-down process dominated by politicians, bankers, and technology vendors. Smart cities should mirror modern societies, which tend to be flatter, more egalitarian, and less rigidly hierarchical than Industrial Age societies.

Like most modern societies, smart cities will be looser, more flexible, and more self-organizing than traditional patriarchal societies. There's no rule that says smart cities have to function like socialist states of the 20th century. A smart city can encourage and support a culture that places high value on traits, such as independence, ruggedness, innovation, and personal responsibility. It's possible that smart-city dwellers will have more in common with prehistoric hunters and gatherers than with people living in tightly organized agricultural or industrial societies.

We can only guess at what life was like for our gritty ancestors; it seems as if they used every bit of whatever they caught or found. Like them, smart-city dwellers will become relentless recyclers and reusers. Doubtlessly, concerted efforts by cities to encourage recycling and to enforce recycling rules will offend some citizens. They'll just have to get over it.

The alternative to ruthless recycling is the traditional *take, make, waste* economic model in which people blithely assume there will be everlasting and inexhaustible supplies of basic natural resources, such as air, water, trees, and minerals. Cities of the future will operate more like space stations, which are essentially closed systems with finite resources. Instead of *take, make, waste,* smart cities will *take, use, return.*

Today, most cities remain insatiably hungry consumers of material and energy. Smart cities will follow the precepts and practices of the circular economy, a model popularized by the Ellen MacArthur Foundation,[3] the US Green Building Council,[4] and other organizations concerned about sustainability, climate change, and growing threats to the environment. In *Waste to Wealth: The Circular Economy Advantage,* authors Peter Lacy and Jacob Rutqvist[5] describe circular strategies as the intentional "decoupling of economic growth" from the wasteful and ultimately self-destructive consumption of constrained natural resources such as fossil fuels, clean water, hardwood forests, and precious metals.

By their calculations, the traditional linear growth model pursued by human beings since the beginning of the Industrial Revolution[6] is slowly grinding to a halt and slipping into reverse gear. They foresee a looming gap of 8 billion tons "between supply and demand for constrained natural resources." They predict the gap will translate into "$4.5 trillion of lost growth by 2030, ballooning to $25 trillion in by 2050."

If their calculations are correct, most people won't have to worry about overconsumption because pretty soon there won't be much of anything left to consume—and whatever is left around will be prohibitively expensive. Our reliance on take-make-waste economics has taken us to the edge of the cliff. We can jump off like lemmings, or choose another path.[7]

Smart cities are blazing the trail toward a new era of sustainable growth by adopting principles of circular and sharing economics. For example, a key tenet of circular economics is replacing products with services as primary outputs of economic activity. In addition to becoming ruthless recyclers of goods and materials, smart cities will become serial innovators and inventors of new services. They will also adopt the principles of sharing economies, in which resources such as cars, condos, and electric bicycles are shared among several owners.

There are many good reasons for smart cities to focus on the development and delivery of innovative services. Here are three:

1. Services require fewer material resources to develop and deploy.

2. Innovation plays to a core strength of smart cities: their ability to attract bright, imaginative, and creative people.

3. Within the next couple of decades if not sooner, almost all manufacturing jobs will be performed by next-generation industrial robots, which are generally smaller, lighter, smarter, more agile, and much less expensive than the current generation of industrial robots. It's unconscionable for politicians to talk about the return of good manufacturing jobs, because most of those jobs aren't coming back. Jobs requiring repetitive tasks will be automated, which means that robots, not humans, will be doing the work.

Robotic workers will become the norm in construction and manufacturing. They will repair our streets, roads, bridges, and buildings. Robots will become the familiar sights. They will operate machinery, inspect utility infrastructure, repair potholes, clear storm drains, and probably even walk our dogs. In Japan, robots are already caring for the elderly.

Robots will become fungible commodities. They will be manufactured and assembled in suburban or exurban industrial zones, shipped to cities, and programmed by creative city dwellers. The valuable part of a robot will be its programming, not its metal or plastic body. And most of all, what matters is how robots will support and augment the quality of life of city dwellers.

The Future of Work Is the Future of Cities

Programming a robot or thinking up new tasks for robots to perform will be creative work. It won't be done in factories or in laboratories. It will be done in shared work spaces that are popping up in cities all over the world. Those shared work spaces are another key element of the emerging smart-city landscape.

"In cities, there are lots of bright people looking for places to sit down and work. Smart cities will encourage the development of shared work spaces that can become incubators for startup and new businesses," Hultin says. "Talented people need places where they feel comfortable, where diversity is appreciated, and where they aren't feeling judged or marginalized for being different."

Encouraging shared work spaces and start-up incubators seems like an easy way for cities to attract people with the talent, energy, and creativity needed to compete successfully in the 21st-century global economy.

We interviewed Hultin in a small conference room at the Hub@GCT, a 50,000-square-foot multipurpose innovation center near Grand Central Station in Midtown Manhattan. The Hub@GCT opened in 2016 as a shared work space for growth-stage (post-seed, and Series A and B funding) software and so-called urbantech companies. It has a Silicon-Valley-meets-Princeton-University kind of vibe—an unexpected combination of relaxed comfort, cool efficiency, youthful energy, and high-octane brainpower.

When we asked Hultin to describe what the future of work and commerce would look like, he looked around and said, "Places like this."

The Hub@GCT is one of several initiatives launched by Urbantech NYC, an offshoot of the New York City Economic Development Corporation. Urbantech NYC, according to its website, is "a comprehensive entrepreneurship ecosystem that catalyzes innovation and supports entrepreneurs making cities more sustainable, resilient, and livable." Its objective is "to increase access to talent and resources, provide transparency and fluidity, and promote New York City urbantech ingenuity globally."

With its laid-back ambiance and Zen-like décor, the Hub@GCT embodies the zeitgeist. But if there's a rock star of the urban shared work space movement, it's WeWork.

WeWork manages roughly 10 million square feet of office space in 23 US cities and 21 countries. The company is valued at about $20 billion, "putting it in a league with Palantir and SpaceX as the most highly valued private US tech start-ups after Airbnb and Uber," writes Jessi Hempel in Wired.[8]

WeWork was founded in 2010 by Adam Neumann and Miguel McKelvey. Both founders deeply understand the physics and psychology of shared spaces—Neumann grew up on a kibbutz in Israel and McKelvey "was raised in a five-mother commune in Eugene, Oregon," according to his *Forbes* profile.[9] Before founding WeWork, the pair had founded Green Desk, an "eco-friendly co-workspace"[10] in the hip DUMBO section of Brooklyn.

It is possible to view WeWork's business model as an extremely clever way of exploiting soft, urban, real estate markets; but that would be missing the point. WeWork *is* clever and financially astute, yet its success rides on a keen awareness of how digital technology and the rise of social networks have fundamentally altered the nature of work. WeWork spaces are designed and furnished to feel more like living spaces and less like office spaces.

The typical WeWork space suggests a fraternity or sorority house with nice modern furniture, tasteful carpets, carefully tended plants, Wi-Fi, and a reception desk in front. For people who hate traditional offices WeWork is a paradise, with amenities like fresh-fruit water, microroasted coffee, and craft beer on tap. Even large corporations with major investments in suburban office parks are shifting workers to shared urban spaces.

There are financial incentives, too. At WeWork, a startup or small business with four employees saves on average $18,000 a year, compared with rent for a traditional private office. Startups and small businesses at WeWork have a 12 percent higher three-year survival rate than their peers, according to the company's blog.[11]

The blog also cites a study on shared work space by Emergent Research, Office Nomads, and Global Coworking Unconference Conference, in which 84 percent of respondents said they were more engaged and motivated when co-working, 82 percent said co-working had expanded their professional networks, 67 percent said co-working had improved their professional success, and 69 percent said they felt more successful since joining a co-working space.

Shared work spaces also provide emotional benefits and relief from the sense of isolation experienced by many city dwellers. According to the study, 89 percent of respondents reported that they were happier, 83 percent reported that they were less lonely, and 78 percent reported that "coworking (sic) helps keep them sane."[12]

Workforce Transformation

From McKelvey's perspective, the "me decade" has evolved into the "we decade"—a time of people coming together and working collaboratively. Cities will play a major role in the societal shift, and companies such as WeWork see themselves as agents of change on a global scale.

Changing demographics have transformed urban millennials into a force of nature. WeWork seems aware of both the irony and the opportunity. Here are brief snippets from the company's landing page: [13]

> *The year 2007 marked the first time in human history that a majority of the Earth's population lived in cities. By 2050 it will be over 70 percent, and by 2020 a majority of the workforce will be millennials. Where will we live, work, and play?*

People are moving to cities, seeking community, purpose, and the opportunity to create their life's work. There has been a macro shift toward a new way of working and living—people are focused on meaningful connections and being part of something greater than themselves.

WeWork is surfing a giant wave of change. Cities are becoming the main engines of the world's economies,[14] and soon the majority of people will live in cities. The economic and demographic trends are inescapable. Ready or not, we're becoming an urban planet, a world of cities.

The best of those cities will also be the smartest and the most adaptable. The shining cities of the future will listen to their citizens and learn from them. They will use technology and data science to continually improve the quality of services they offer. They will become powerful attractors of innovative, inventive, and imaginative people.

"Smart cities will be environments where people can find work, raise families, innovate and create, and enjoy life. Smart cities will look beyond simply maintaining what they already have; they will look ahead to reshaping their destinies, learning to provide the resources necessary for their citizens to excel, and sharing their knowledge as broadly as possible. At their core, smart cities learn how to improve the quality of life of their citizens. Smart cities increase the odds that we, as the human species, not only survive, but thrive as the future unfolds," Hultin says.

Endnotes

1. Charles Lindbergh's solo flight across the Atlantic in 1927 was dismissed by many as a publicity stunt, but it raised the image of aviation from a carnival attraction to a practical mode of transportation, and it set the stage for commercial trans-Atlantic flights.

2. https://council.nyc.gov/press/2017/06/06/1426

3. https://www.ellenmacarthurfoundation.org/circular-economy/overview/concept

4. https://new.usgbc.org/about

5. *Waste to Wealth: The Circular Economy Advantage,* Peter Lacy and Jacob Rutqvist.

6. Some might reasonably argue that our current linear growth model emerged 6,000 years ago with the emergence of large agricultural societies and their creation myths, which reinforce the belief that human beings have divinely invested rights to rule over the natural world.

7. We're resisting the urge to call the smart-city movement a "paradigm shift," because the term is both overused and often misunderstood. Paradigm shifts are genuine revolutions in which traditional systems are replaced by dramatically novel systems. The American Revolution, the French Revolution, the theory of relativity, and the discovery of quantum mechanics are examples of true paradigm shifts.

8. https://www.wired.com/story/this-is-why-wework-thinks-its-worth-20-billion

9. https://www.forbes.com/profile/miguel-mckelvey

10. http://www.nydailynews.com/life-style/real-estate/wework-alternative-working-home-swanky-buildings-nyc-article-1.1044412

11. https://www.wework.com/blog/posts/wework-creates-an-economic-ripple-effect-for-cities

12. http://www.smallbizlabs.com/2015/05/coworking-spaces-are-human-spaces.html

13. https://futureofwork.wework.com/?ref=fow

14. https://www.mckinsey.com/global-themes/urbanization/urban-world-mapping-the-economic-power-of-cities

Chapter 5

Human-Centered Design

HUMAN-CENTERED DESIGN is a method for developing products and services based on the observed needs and desires of people. Human-centered design starts by envisioning problems facing people—such as hailing a cab, choosing a doctor, or applying for a job—and then works backward to solve them, always keeping the end user in mind.

It's the opposite of the mad scientist scenario, in which a solitary genius working in a laboratory comes up with a revolutionary invention at midnight and unleashes it on an unsuspecting world.

It's similar to design thinking, service design, and agile development, which also emphasize outcomes and impact over strict adherence to a traditional step-by-step methodology.

What separates human-centered design from other approaches is its specific focus on the user experience.

Smart cities use human-centered design to flip the traditional model of city government on its head. Instead of catering to bureaucrats, politicians, and special interests, they focus on serving residents. They use human-centered design for managing problems and continually improving city services.

Human-centered design begins by looking closely at how people behave in real life and then designing services around their needs. It enables cities to roll out prototypes, measure outcomes, fail fast, and iterate rapidly. With human-centered design, the processes of innovation and improvement never officially end—they are ongoing.

For Matt Klein, human-centered design enables "evidence-based policymaking" and "allocating funds to programs that make a difference."

Klein is executive director of the New York City Mayor's Office for Economic Opportunity (NYC Opportunity) and a senior adviser in the Mayor's Office of Operations. NYC Opportunity's mission is reducing poverty and increasing equity by applying modern tools of research, data science, and design to city programs.

"We want to fund programs that work and stop funding programs that don't work," he says. "Accomplishing our goals requires research, rigorous performance management, continuous evaluation, and real discipline. Sitting around a table and talking is okay, but lots of ideas don't work out as you expect. Our design methodology gives us tools for approaching problems from the perspective of real people and understanding what's going on, so we can be more effective. It's about thinking with data and using data to get better results."

Targeting Hard Problems

Instead of relying on hunches and gut instinct, smart cities use human-centered design to deploy, test, and refine services on a continual basis (Figure 5.1). It's a scientific approach to problem-solving, based on observation and data rather than hearsay or guesswork.

Klein's team helps the city target hard problems that resist traditional solutions. For example, helping low-income residents finish college programs is a common challenge for

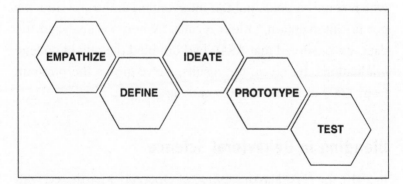

Figure 5.1 Design thinking process steps
Source: Hasso Plattner Institute of Design at Stanford.

local government. "People with a two-year college degree are much less likely to live in poverty. So we want to keep folks in college until they graduate. But the noncompletion rate for first-generation, low-income students is extremely high," Klein explains.

Over the years, New York City has launched a number of initiatives to boost the completion rate. The most successful of the initiatives is the City University of New York's Accelerated Study in Associate Programs (ASAP),[1] which employs a variety of tactics to help students stay in college. Some of the tactics involve extra counseling, personal advice, and help with course work. Some are even simpler, such as waiving mandatory college fees and providing free rides on public transit, so students can travel more easily to their classes.

ASAP didn't evolve randomly. "The program began as a pilot with 1,000 students as a test. We performed a number of different evaluations, including a randomized control trial in which some students got the intervention and some students got no intervention," Klein recalls. "When we analyzed the data, we observed that ASAP had doubled the rate of college graduations. Based on the results, we've grown the program from 1,000 to nearly 25,000 students."

Blending in Behavioral Science

In 2016, the NYC Mayor's Office of Operations partnered with ideas42, a behavioral design firm, to create the Behavioral

Design Team (BDT), a first for the city. "We draw insight from behavioral science to design a variety of inexpensive and scalable interventions," Klein explains.

For example, behavioral science shows that the desire to hold on to what you already have is stronger than the desire to gain something new. "It's called 'loss aversion' and it's an aspect of human behavior we can utilize to keep people from losing their benefits," Klein says.

Filling out the annual Free Application for Federal Student Aid (FAFSA) form, for instance, is difficult and time consuming. Nevertheless, it's necessary if you want to receive financial aid for college, and it must be filled out every year that you apply for aid. Most high schools provide help for students who have trouble filling out the FAFSA form. After they're in college, the students are expected to fill out the form on their own, and therein lies the problem. Many students don't fill out the form, and as a result, they lose their financial aid and drop out of college.

The BDT developed an intervention program to increase FAFSA filing rates at three CUNY campuses. The results were carefully monitored and measured. Filing rates increased at all three campuses, rising 38.18 percent at the Borough of Manhattan Community College, 19.79 percent at Bronx Community College, and 28.06 percent at Hostos Community College. Based on the results, CUNY decided to expand the program to the majority of its two-year community colleges in the city.

The city also tries to prevent Supplemental Nutrition Assistance Program (SNAP) recipients from losing their benefits. "SNAP requires families to recertify periodically. If they don't recertify, they fall off the rolls. Reapplying from scratch is a more cumbersome process and it's more expensive for the city to administer," Klein explains. "And the family is without that nutritional assistance in the meantime."

An intervention developed by the BDT for a trial group of 20,000 SNAP recipients reduced the rate of failure for submitting a required form by 5.5 percent and led to an increase of 12.9 percent for form submission during the first 45 days of the recertification period, according to the city.

"Small differences in the design or context of processes, programs, and services can influence how people make decisions and take action—or don't," Klein explains. "Behavioral science applications, which are often quick and inexpensive to implement, can improve the effectiveness of programs and policies."

When families are on the verge of losing nutritional benefits, the city can send customized "nudges" via text or email, reminding them to recertify. "We do A/B tests, sending a message to one group of residents and a different message to another group. Again, we test rigorously with randomized control groups," Klein says. "In some cases, we're not doing a new or expensive intervention. We're simply rewriting a message or adding another layer of communication. As a result, recertification rates go up."

The BDT recently worked with the Fire Department of New York (FDNY) to increase its diversity. The team conducted a randomized control trial to determine if waiving filing fees for applicants would increase the diversity of applicants taking the FDNY's qualifying examination.

The trial, which involved a subset of applicants, showed that waiving the fees increased filing rates for FDNY's new-recruit applications by 36.7 percent overall, with an 84 percent increase among black candidates and an 83 percent increase among female candidates, according to the city.

Bringing Together Data and Design

New York City took a major step toward institutionalizing the concepts of human-centered design in 2017 when it launched the Service Design Studio. The studio is a public-private partnership, financed by city government and Citi Community Development,[2] an arm of Citigroup that promotes financial inclusion and economic empowerment for underserved individuals, families, and communities across the United States.

Composed of city employees with professional backgrounds in design, the studio functions as a citywide resource delivering projects in collaboration with agencies and drawing on NYC Opportunity's product managers, software developers, business analysts, content analysts, and community liaisons.

Infusing city projects and initiatives with human-centric design principles is not an easy task; governments have a long tradition of resisting good design. But the studio has a special arrow in its quiver: data science.

In addition to creating apps, webpages and online forms that are functional, secure, and look great from a design perspective, the studio also tests its products for usability in the field. After the products have been released, the team continually gathers data, monitors performance, identifies problems, and makes tweaks or updates to ensure optimal usability.

"We're looking at data almost in real time to see what's happening," says Ariel Kennan, the studio's first director. "Anytime we make an adjustment to any of the products, we're building lightweight prototypes and testing. In addition to the test data, we're also getting feedback from individual users."

The studio recently created the *Tools & Tactics* guide to formalize best practices and provide general design advice for other city agencies (Figure 5.2). "We're adding to the toolbox," says Kennan. The studio also hosts hands-on workshops and events for designers and developers working for other city agencies.

Additionally, the studio supports an informal citywide push to replace technical jargon with easy-to-understand language across a variety of platforms, products, and user endpoints.

"We've done a lot of work on how we communicate about city programs and how we make them easier to use," Kennan says. "For example, how do we make sure that we're

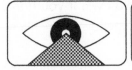

Set the Stage

As you begin to consider creating a new service, or if you're looking to better understand or enhance an existing service, it's helpful to...

Talk with People

Taking time to talk one-on-one or in groups with the people who use, deliver, and govern your service is possibly the most crucial step you...

Connect the Dots

Making sense of what you've seen, heard, and learned is a crucial part of the service design process. Following these few techniques will...

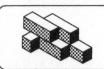

Try Things Out

After listening intently and turning observations into insights, it's now time to brainstorm new ideas and put them into action...

Focus on Impact

Now that you've talked with people, reviewed relevant evidence, and tested some ideas, you have no doubt created a clearer sense of what...

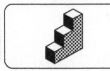

Get More Help

While there are many parts of the service design process you and your team can tackle, you don't always have the capacity to go it alone...

Figure 5.2 NYC Civic Service Design Tools & Tactics
Source: NYC Civic Service Design Studio.

writing in language that's really plain and understandable to you, even if English isn't your primary language?"

For some services, the city translates content into 11 different languages. "We did a big content design exercise where we took information from about 40 programs and created a data standard behind them for all the different elements, then rewrote all of the content in partnership with the agencies to simplify the language," she says. The results of the exercise were shared across the city's agencies and released publicly.[3]

Plain Language

"Government loves to speak in acronyms and use very complicated names," Kennan says. "In our dataset, we have a plain language name for all of our programs. So even if you don't know the official name of the program or agency, you're likely to find it without too much trouble.

For example, the studio has worked with ACCESS NYC,[4] an online eligibility screening tool, to simplify user experiences across New York City's many bureaus, departments, and agencies.

"ACCESS NYC has an eligibility screener on it, so you can enter basic information about you and your family and then determine which programs you may be eligible for," Kennan explains. "The service was a revolutionary use of technology when it was launched in 2006. But it wasn't human centered. So what we were seeing was that people were starting the screener and then not finishing it. We knew just from looking at the data that we had a user-experience problem, and we knew we had to fix it."

The studio built lightweight prototypes and field-tested them. "We went out and tested the prototypes with caseworkers and with residents, and with people who spoke different languages. We made sure that the new version was easy to use and understand," says Kennan. "Since then, we've seen our success rate (finishing the screener) go up by about 25 percent."

Back to the Drawing Board

The path between identifying a problem and fixing it can take unexpected detours. A solution that looks great to a designer can be confusing to a user.

"We did a lot of the up-front testing on ACCESS NYC. One of the things we originally thought was that we would make the site more inviting and less staid. We wanted it to look less like a government site and we thought it needed more graphics," Kennan recalls.

When the studio team tested their new designs, it turned out many people were confused by the graphics. "They didn't know why this government website had pictures on it. From their perspective, it somehow didn't seem trustworthy. It didn't seem to them like something that was coming from a government agency," she says.

The test results were a surprise. Initially, the team assumed they had chosen the wrong images. "We tried a couple of different variations to see if particular graphics were causing the issue. But eventually, we actually removed most of the images on the home page," Kennan says.

Cool graphics aren't always absolutely necessary— sometimes you just need to let the text speak for itself.

"We have some icons that we use elsewhere in the site, but in a more minimalistic way. As designers, we love colorful imagery and playfulness. But sometimes our idea of good design doesn't resonate with the people we're trying to reach," Kennan says.

The studio's experience reveals the strength of human-centered design. When your efforts revolve around real-life human beings, you don't mind going back to the drawing board and rethinking your design. It's all about the user experience. Sometimes designers have to adjust their designs, even when they seem perfect.

The studio's reliance on agile methodology also adds to its strength. Agile methodology, which is used primarily by software developers, is based on continuous testing, iteration, and improvement. The Service Design Studio proves that with a little imagination, "agile" can be applied successfully almost anywhere.

Invisible Heroes

The studio has also partnered with NYC's Department of Homeless Services and street homeless service providers to get a clearer picture of how the city's street homeless utilize city services designed to help them. Here are short excerpts from a post[5] written by the studio describing the project:

> *Street homeless New Yorkers interact with many government agencies and services within any given week, yet many still cycle in and out of care while searching for permanent housing. Our goal was to understand their complete journey from living on the street to being permanently housed, to identify what barriers they and their service providers face, and to create enhancements to improve end-to-end service delivery.*

Kennan and her team clearly aren't afraid to leave their desks and hit the streets to see for themselves how people are using the products they design. Good designers don't just design for themselves; they design for users in the real world.

*With permission from appropriate City agencies, we shad-
owed street outreach workers to understand their processes
and observe their interactions with homeless individuals
and City agencies. This included accompanying some workers on their full overnight shifts. We also visited a Human
Resources Administration (HRA) center to observe part of
the process homeless clients and their case managers may go
through to place them in permanent housing. We also conducted one-on-one interviews and small-group interviews
with staff from providers, government agencies, and clients.*

Here's a key point that could be easily overlooked: Kennan
and her team worked with the service providers to document
the process from end to end. "We actually documented every
single step, from first contact to final placement in permanent
housing," Kennan says. "As we documented the service process, we thought about how we could enhance it. We asked
ourselves and our partners, 'Where are the gaps, where are
the delays, and where are people getting stuck?' Asking those
kinds of questions and carefully documenting the process in
a collaborative effort with the service providers has led to the
development of a new case management system and new
tools for delivering better service."

The real heroes of this story are the people doing homeless outreach work on the streets of New York City, Kennan
says. "They are the invisible heroes working our streets every
single day. They are strong and they are good at what they
do. Documenting and analyzing the steps of their process
enabled us to develop better tools and techniques for helping them deal with the problems of homelessness in a very
large and complex city."

Keeping It Simple

The Service Design Studio issued the list[6] of simple principles summarizing its approach to solving design problems that's shown in Figure 5.3.

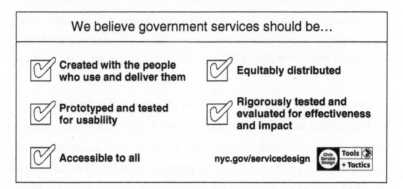

Figure 5.3 NYC Service Design Studio principles
Source: NYC Civic Service Design Studio.

Single Purpose, Many Hats

Kennan is a graduate of the Parsons School of Design, where she studied integrated design with concentrations in digital technology and communications design. Her studies included coursework in typography, digital motion, production, digital screenprint, spatial graphics, interactive design for museums, information design, design research, and sustainable design. After graduating from Parsons, she worked at ESI Design, a major design studio in New York. She was later selected for a Code for America fellowship, which gave her a first-hand view of the challenges and rewards of working with government.

We include the granular details of Kennan's background to highlight the need for multidisciplinary experience. One of the many lessons we've learned over the course of researching and writing this book is that smart cities need people like Kennan—energetic and energizing leaders who are comfortable shuttling back and forth between various domains, crossing turf boundaries, and wearing many hats.

"It is scary sometimes," Kennan says. "How do we break down barriers? How do we reduce conflict around things? How do we work through the challenges and actually make it a collaborative process, bringing together insights from people who deliver and use our services? How do we make our services more equitable? How do make sure things are really fair? How do we operate more efficiently? How do we make sure that we're spending taxpayer dollars responsibly?"

Kennan says the continuous feedback loop informs every decision made by the studio and prevents it from losing its focus. "I see us as smart public servants of the 21st century. We have a mission, and we're monitoring the results of our work every single day to make better and smarter choices."

Designing for Usability

Smart cities don't just provide services for their citizens; they provide services that citizens actually use. Services must be accessible and understandable. They must overcome barriers of language and culture. They cannot merely exist; they need to present an attractive value proposition. Each and every city service must send an unambiguous message: *I am useful. Use me and I will help you.*

"If you build it, they will come"[7] is not a strategy. The success or failure of a smart-city service depends on its usability. If you're a New York City subway rider, you've undoubtedly seen the ceramic plaques and intricate mosaic tile designs decorating the walls of many older stations. When the subway opened in 1904, those plaques and tiles weren't intended solely for decorative purposes. The designers included them to make sure that even if you were illiterate or couldn't read English, you could still find your way around the subway system.

Good design is a fundamental part of usability. If the mobile, online, or printed version of an application form for a city service doesn't look appealing, if it looks too complicated or too daunting, if there's something about it that doesn't look quite right, people simply won't use it.

One of the reasons we love our smart phones is because they look cool. The smart phone is perhaps the most obvious example of well-designed technology that is useful, elegant, and easy to operate. City services should be more like smart phones; if you feel that you need a lawyer to help you figure out how to use a service, there's a good chance that it's poorly designed. On the other hand, if you feel that using a service or applying for a benefit is a no-brainer, you should probably thank whomever designed the user interface.

Endnotes

1. http://www1.cuny.edu/sites/asap/

2. http://citicommunitydevelopment.com/citi/citizen/community/

3. http://on.nyc.gov/benefitsapi

4. http://www1.nyc.gov/nyc-resources/service/4866/access-nyc

5. https://civicservicedesign.com/home-stat-cb33905555b9

6. https://civicservicedesign.com/service-design-principles-c763f64ac950

7. The actual line whispered to Kevin Costner's character in the 1989 motion picture *Field of Dreams* is, "If you build it, he will come."

Chapter 6

Citizens in the Loop

TEL AVIV is a city that radiates energy and enthusiasm. It often seems to vibrate at its own unique frequency, like a rare subatomic particle in a physics experiment.

The name itself reflects the city's embrace of the new and the ancient. *Tel* is commonly translated as "hill," but it refers to a mound created by successive layers of archeological ruins. It's a tangible reminder of the past. *Aviv* means "spring," the season of rebirth and renewal.

Tel Aviv is simultaneously exotic and familiar. You can party in its many bars and nightclubs, swim in the Mediterranean, stretch out on its sandy beaches, hike through the hills, and relax in its parks. Tel Aviv calls itself "Nonstop City," a nickname that nicely captures the city's hectic pace.

But Tel Aviv can be a challenging place to live, especially if you're a secular middle-class citizen with a family. It can be difficult to find family-friendly activities that don't cost a fortune or require long rides. Parts of the city shut down on Friday afternoon for Sabbath and remain closed through Saturday evening.

Eytan Schwartz was born on Manhattan's Upper East Side and moved to Tel Aviv with his family when he was 7 years old. After graduating from Columbia University, he returned to Tel Aviv, where he lives with his wife and their three young children.

"We live in the center of the city and we don't have a car," he says. "So we look for activities we can walk to with the kids. There's a lot going on around us, but it's hard to know where and when something is happening nearby. That's why I like DigiTel, because it shows me free or inexpensive activities that are geared to families."

DigiTel is Tel Aviv's citizen information platform (Figure 6.1). It was conceived and designed by local government to keep citizens engaged and informed. Nearly two-thirds of the city's eligible residents (age 13 or older) are registered to use the platform, which provides "individually tailored, location-specific, life-situation-based information and services."[1]

For example, if you're the parent of young children, you can use DigiTel to find the nearest events or activities for young children. "There's a beautiful pool in the square near our apartment," Schwartz says. "People bring their radio-controlled model boats and sail them around the pool.

Figure 6.1 DigiTel information platform
Source: DigiTel.

DigiTel texts me a link to an offer for a free boat for the kids. I sign up, we walk over to the pool, we put our boat in the water and the kids are happy for two hours. That's very cool."

Recently, the city began hosting free dance parties for parents and their children on Saturday afternoons. "The city sends out notices on DigiTel, brings over a couple of DJs, and everybody has a good time. The parties are in business neighborhoods, so nobody minds the loud music. And the businesses love it because it brings them more traffic," Schwartz says. "As a citizen, the overall impression I get is that somebody cares for me, somebody is catering to me."

Tel Aviv residents also use DigiTel to apply for permits and licenses, find bargain rates at parking lots, sign up for classes and activities, get discounts on concert tickets, avoid road construction, and remember when it's time to register their children for school. For Tel Aviv residents, it's a convenient utility.

"I'm not a tech person. I'm not really interested in technology. I don't have the patience for upgrading devices and downloading software. DigiTel serves my needs as a city resident, which is why I use it," Schwartz says.

Weaving a Stronger Social Fabric

DigiTel is an example of bottom-up innovation. It wasn't part of a grand plan or strategy. It arose from an issue confronting city governments all over the world: most citizens, no matter where they live, dislike government. For many of us, government feels more like a source of problems than a wellspring of solutions. We associate local government with parking fines, speeding tickets, tax bills, cracked sidewalks, potholes, and lack of parking spaces.

The mastermind behind DigiTel is Zohar Sharon, a former social worker who envisioned a platform for bringing together citizens and city government. Instead of allowing technology to divide and isolate people, the city would use it to weave a stronger social fabric.

Sharon is Tel Aviv's chief knowledge officer. "I'm responsible for knowledge and information, not for technology," he explains. "From our point of view, technology is a means to an end. It helps us build connections between citizens and their city."

When Sharon took the job in 2006, he saw an immediate issue: Most of the information that citizens needed was stored in separate data silos. Each unit of city government had its own silo and its own data. Each unit also had its own web pages on the city website, which made it difficult for citizens to find information. The pages were updated haphazardly; important information was often missing or outdated. As a result, the website itself became a source of irritation, adding to a general attitude of cynicism and negativity about city government.

"We held focus groups with citizens and asked two questions: What do you think about Tel Aviv and what do you think about the city government of Tel Aviv? City managers and officials watched through a one-way mirror as people responded to the questions," he recalls.

The responses were shattering. The citizens said they loved Tel Aviv, but hated the city government. "We were shocked," Sharon says. "We provided great services and the people still thought we were terrible. We were in real pain."

One of Sharon's first tasks was streamlining and improving the city's website. "Citizens want to go to the website and find the information they need. Instead, they would find photos of the department managers and detailed descriptions of how the various units were organized. Nobody cares about that stuff, so we got rid of it," he says.

The city rebuilt and redesigned the website "from the citizen's perspective," Sharon says. It removed the clutter and made it easier for citizens to find information with the least possible effort. "When people are looking for information, they want to find it fast."

Sharon's key insight was the centrality of the citizen experience in the development of a citywide information service. He also wasn't afraid to craft a practical solution using standard tools and technologies. There's nothing in Tel Aviv's municipal website that a software engineer would find especially exciting. But Sharon's goal wasn't to create something exciting—it just had to be better than the city's existing website.

Trained as a social worker, it was natural for Sharon to focus on the people first and the technology second. His approach wasn't groundbreaking or revolutionary, but it illustrates an essential quality of genuinely smart cities: They elevate people over technology.

Transitioning to a people-centered strategy doesn't happen overnight. Tel Aviv's approach followed a pattern that has become familiar in the business world: Early versions of information platforms reflect the desires of technologists and later versions reflect the desires of users.

It's commonly said that digital transformation involves people, processes, and technology. What's often left out of the formula is leadership. Every transformation needs leaders: people with the vision, energy, and patience to make it all happen. Sharon knew that his transformation plan would need leaders, so he created a small army of them.

Knowledge Champions

Organizations have multiple stakeholders and constituencies. There are dueling egos, ongoing turf wars, and endless battles for limited resources. Leaders of transformational initiatives must step carefully across numerous functional areas, levels of management, and layers of bureaucracy.

Early on, Sharon had to win over the city employees who fed information into the city's website. "We quickly realized that if we wanted a good information platform, we would need good information," he says. That meant constantly adding and updating information, which required extra work by city employees.

It was relatively easy to create a platform with the technical capabilities for serving a small city. The hard part was creating a program of incentives that would keep city workers sufficiently motivated to continually add and update relevant information on a voluntary basis with minimal supervision.

Even in Israel, where the sense of shared responsibility is unusually high, people don't like to do extra work. There has to be some kind of motivation. Here's where Sharon's social skills came in handy. He recruited 250 city employees to serve as *knowledge champions*. They assumed the mantle of responsibility for updating and adding information to the website.

The champions receive special training and recognition for their efforts. They are among the first to use the city's newest technology tools. "There are many ways to incentivize people without spending lots of money," says Sharon. "The champions feel good because their work has a positive impact on thousands of city residents. Those good feelings are an incentive."

The knowledge champions have become an elite corps within the city government's 8,000-person workforce. They also play a subtle but important role in improving the operations of city government. "Because they are from departments all over the city, they help us break down the silos. We share information more easily now, which makes us more effective as a city government," says Sharon.

Start-Up Government

Sharon's successful effort to improve the city's online presence led to another idea: Why not create a web and mobile platform for Tel Aviv residents who are looking for city services and activities that match their interests based on age, family status, and location?

He recalls pitching the idea of DigiTel as a start-up rather than as a typical government program. "I remember saying to my boss that we need to look at the city as a circle of life. Different people are in different parts of the circle. When you have young children, you focus on your family. When you're older, you want to go places, meet people and travel."

Instead of serving the same information to everyone, DigiTel would follow the example of successful digital businesses and enable users to create personalized experiences based on their individual needs and preferences. Sharon's approach was modeled on firmly established digital marketing principles. For a city government, however, it was revolutionary.

"With DigiTel, we can send targeted messages to the right people, at the right time, and at the right place," says Sharon. "For example, if you're the parent of a 5-year-old and there's a concert for children at the community center in your neighborhood tomorrow, we'll send you a text and let you know about it."

DigiTel will also text you if there are seats available at popular shows. "If you request them, we'll send you alerts when half-price tickets are available for tonight's shows," he says. "It's a win-win situation because more people get to see the shows and the theaters fill their seats. Fifteen minutes before show time, there are no empty theater seats in Tel Aviv."

The success of DigiTel led to the creation of two more platforms: DigiTaf, a platform for parents of preschool children, and DigiDog, a platform for dog owners. With 20,000 registered dogs, Tel Aviv has a higher canine-to-human ratio than any other city in the world. DigiDog provides dog owners with personalized information about pet-friendly events, vaccination reminders, nearby veterinary services, locations of dog parks, and discounts at pet stores.

Following Instincts, Not Tech Trends

Tel Aviv is a city that nurtures and encourages technology innovation. It's been described as "Silicon Valley on the Mediterranean." It's a city of startups in a startup nation.

But DigiTel isn't state-of-the-art technology. It represents something more important: a victory for local government. It shows you don't have to be a genius backed by a group of venture capitalists to create a service that improves lives across a modern city; you can be a civil servant with good instincts and the willingness to tinker with the status quo.

DigiTel has turned Sharon into a celebrity of the world-wide smart-cities movement. He's become an unofficial ambassador for Tel Aviv, traveling the world and sharing the DigiTel story with enraptured audiences. When he talks, he sounds like the manager of a small business explaining basic concepts, such as employee motivation and customer satisfaction. He doesn't obsess over software and hardware.

A fundamental part of Sharon's success was his ability to imbue city workers with the belief that their work was important and meaningful to the people of Tel Aviv. "The biggest thing we did was change the internal culture in our unit of government. We changed the way our workers were thinking about their jobs. They feel an emotional connection now. They feel they're helping people. That's a powerful incentive."

Endnote

1. http://zoharsharon.blogspot.com

Chapter 7

We Decide

BARCELONA IS a pioneer in the smart-cities movement. The city's annual Smart City Expo World Congress has become a major international trade show, attracting tens of thousands of attendees and hundreds of companies.

The city had spent years and millions of euros implementing a top-down strategy for transforming itself into a smart city. But when the strategy produced meager results, Barcelona replaced it with an approach that prioritizes the voices of citizens in the city's planning processes.

Instead of focusing primarily on technology, Barcelona expanded its definition of a smart city to include smart government and smart citizens.

In many respects, the new approach is genuinely revolutionary. It doesn't merely offer opportunities for citizens to get involved—it creates a collaborative ecosystem for reinventing democracy in the digital age.

"Modern democracy needs the support of modern technology," says Gala Pin Ferrando, a political activist elected to the Barcelona City Council in 2015.

In 2016, the city council launched Decidim, a public digital platform for participatory democracy. Decidim enables citizens to submit ideas, keep track of ongoing initiatives, and review proposals submitted online or in person at meetings of city officials.[1]

Developed at Barcelona's Laboratory for Democratic Innovation, Decidim is a joint effort of 17 organizations, including software companies, industry consortiums, research institutions, and civic associations.

"Decidim allows citizens to propose ideas, conduct surveys, call public meetings, and join the debate on whether proposals are good solutions to identified needs," Pin explains. "Decidim enables government to know which proposals have the most support from citizens. Overall, it makes democracy better."

As of spring 2018, Decidim Barcelona "had more than 28,000 registered participants; 1,288,999 page views; 290,520 visitors; 19 participatory processes; 821 public meetings channeled through the platform; and 12,173 proposals, out of which over 8,923 have already become public policies grouped into 5,339 results whose execution level can be monitored by citizens," according to the Decidim website.[2] In addition to Barcelona, Decidim is currently used by municipalities in other parts of Spain and by local governments in Finland and France.

Updating Democracy

Decidim, which means "we decide" in Catalan, was born from a series of protests that coalesced in 2011 as Spain's 15-M movement, a nationwide grassroots effort to replace the country's top-down governing system with something more fundamentally democratic.

"The systems of representative democracy used across Europe were invented 200 years ago when people traveled on horses," says Xabier E. Barandiaran Fernández, director and coordinator of the Decidim project.

Government proceeded at a leisurely pace because it took weeks for information and ideas to circulate across a country. If you had an idea to propose, you had to saddle up your horse, ride to the nearest government capital, and hope someone in a position of influence would listen to your idea.

Ordinary citizens didn't have the time to attend government meetings, so they sent elected representatives. The forms of representative democracy that emerged after the French Revolution were certainly better than feudalism. But they were far from perfect.

The rise of modern digital information and communication technology has put the traditional processes of representative democracy under new scrutiny. "Democracy needs an update," says Barandiaran. "Democracy is more than just voting every four years and putting your democratic rights into other people's hands."

For a brief period of time, it seemed as if commercial social media networks, such as Facebook and Twitter, might serve as alternatives or adjuncts to some aspects of traditional democracy. It's clear now that privately owned social networks aren't set up to sustain the complicated processes of public governance.

"In the early stages of a social movement, platforms like Facebook and Twitter can be very helpful because they help people to connect. You don't have to be a technology expert or a web designer to spread your message," Barandiaran says. "But those platforms are big businesses. Their goals are commoditizing social interactions and making money."

From the perspective of the social activists in Barcelona, it made sense for the city itself to create a digital platform enabling a new mode of democracy.

"Decidim is a digital infrastructure for participatory democracy, built entirely and collaboratively as free software," Barandiaran says. The code for Decidim is posted on GitHub, the popular hosting service for open-source software projects.[3] "Decidim allows any organization (local city council, association, university, NGO, neighborhood, or cooperative) to create mass processes for strategic planning, participatory budgeting, collaborative design for regulations, urban spaces, and election processes."

Additionally, it supports traditional in-person democratic meetings (e.g., assemblies, town halls, and council meetings) by sending meeting invites, managing registrations, streaming content, and facilitating the publication of minutes. Decidim also enables registered participants and member organizations to convene referendums and trigger decision-making processes for proposals and initiatives.

Barandiaran also leads MetaDecidim, a community of more than 300 registered users from all over the world who design, support, and continuously refine components of the Decidim project.[4] "This is real-time government and we are constantly improving the platform," he says.

Ditch the Status Quo

Barcelona's government shares many similarities with city governments all over the world. But the city of Barcelona has a reputation for going its own way and embracing risk. Barcelona culture blends a strong sense of cosmopolitanism with deeply ingrained working-class ethics. The city is not afraid to ditch the status quo, change course, and try something new.

When the city elected a new administration in 2015, it began re-examining its smart-city programs. The new mayor,

Ada Colau, was a housing activist. She sensed that in addition to saving water and reducing electricity costs, smart-city technologies could be deployed to empower citizens directly and to help them solve everyday problems.

One of her first moves was hiring Francesca Bria as Barcelona's chief technology and digital innovation officer. Bria, a social innovation expert who had led the European Union's D-CENT project on direct democracy and digital currencies, was asked to "rethink the smart city from the ground up,"[5] which essentially meant sorting through Barcelona's numerous technology investments and then determining which were contributing to city life and which were detracting from it.

For example, placing sensors in city parks had cut costs and reduced the consumption of water, which becomes a scarce commodity during hot summer months. But equipping parking spots with electromagnetic sensors to signal drivers when spots were available was less successful. The sensors couldn't tell the difference between parked cars and passing subway trains. Even when spots were empty, the confused sensors sent no signals until the trains had passed.

Top-down government planning tends to generate those kinds of hit-or-miss results, since it often relies on the opinions of consultants promoting the notion that technology can solve any and all problems. Instead of focusing on achieving results, government focuses on buying technology. That approach can lead to wasteful mistakes, as Barcelona discovered.

"We had a lot of data and a lot of dashboards," Bria says. "In the new Barcelona Digital City Strategy[6] we have shifted from a technology-led approach to a citizens-first approach."

The old strategy focused on big data, sensors, and connectivity. The new strategy focuses on sustainability, mobility, affordable housing, energy transition, climate change, participatory democracy and technological sovereignty.

"The ultimate goal is making government more collaborative, participatory, and transparent," Bria says. "We want government services that are more user friendly and intuitive. We want citizens to work with us and to understand the real benefit of public services."

An important step for the city was the creation of Decidim, which puts Barcelona on track for "building a more inclusive and egalitarian city,"[7] one of Bria's principal objectives.

Technopolitics

Decidim is a window into the future of open government and participatory democracy. Somehow, it manages to make the city's bureaucracy seem charming, hip, and approachable. Its architecture and layout follow a logic that digital natives will find familiar and easy to navigate.

"Decidim is more than a technological platform or infrastructure," Barandiaran explains. "We define it as a 'technopolitical project' where legal, political, institutional, practical, social, educational, communicative, economic, and epistemic codes merge together. Ultimately, Decidim is in itself a sort of crossroad of the various dimensions of networked democracy and society, a detailed practical map of their complexities and conflicts."

Most important, Decidim creates the foundation for a scientific approach to city government. It's an engine for collecting, organizing, and distributing information. It enables citywide crowdsourcing of answers to questions that modern cities have wrestled with for decades: Which neighborhoods should be rebuilt? Which should be torn down? Which parks need better lighting at night? Where should we dig new sewers? Which parts of town need more public transit? Which streets need more frequent cleaning?

Moreover, Decidim allows for continual scoring and evaluation of ongoing projects and processes. It holds a magnifying lens over city government, making it easier for citizens, city officials, and vendors to see which projects are on time, which are behind, and which need to be redesigned or rethought.

Collaborative Government

Decidim covers two broad segments of city planning: PAM (Municipal Action Plan) and PAD (District Action Plan). Within each segment are plans and projects in various stages of progress. Each project has a timeline divided into stages:

1. Information and data collection

2. Diagnosis of needs, defining goals, and objectives

3. Citizen debate

4. Voting to prioritize proposals

5. Follow-up

6. Sharing results and outcomes

The level of execution of the projects is monitored along five dimensions:

1. Good Living

2. Global Justice

3. Plural Economy

4. Ecological Transition

5. Good Governance

Each of the five dimensions includes multiple criteria. Within the Good Living dimension, for example, are Social Justice; Personal Autonomy; Education and Knowledge; Gender Equity and Sexual Diversity; Life Cycles; Housing; Health; Migration, Interculturality, and Zero Discrimination; Defense and Protection of Human Rights; Culture; Sports; and Coexistence and Security (Figure 7.1).

The abundance of criteria serves an important purpose. Each criterion represents a set of data points that can be measured, evaluated, and compared over time. Instead of saying, "It seems like the protection of human rights is a rising concern," you can look at the data and see for yourself.

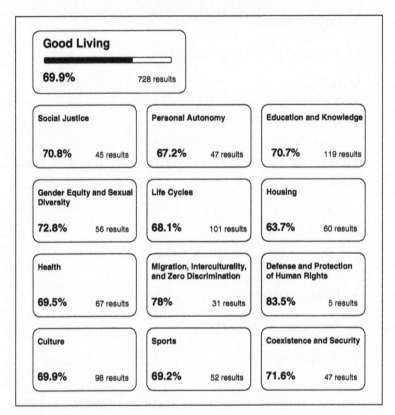

Figure 7.1 Levels of project execution resulting from the participatory process
Source: Decidim Barcelona.

The numerous criteria also function as a kind of shout-out to groups that have been ignored by government in the past. Having multiple criteria makes it harder to overlook or exclude segments of the city population from the collaborative process.

Decidim also minimizes the squeaky-wheel effect, the bane of local governments everywhere. By standardizing and scoring multiple criteria, Decidim opens government planning processes to a far wider range of citizens than ever before.

For example, Barcelona has a history of animal rights activism. The Catalan Parliament voted to ban bullfighting in 2010. Spain's constitutional court overturned the ban in 2016, but Mayor Colau vowed that the city would continue protecting bulls from mistreatment or harm.[8]

The following year, the platform ZOOXXI submitted its first citizens' initiative and posted on the Decidim website. The goal of the initiative is to apply 21st-century standards of humane treatment to the animals in the city zoo. ZOOXXI itself is an international proposal promoting the adoption of modern ethics and scientific principles in zoos worldwide.[9]

Here's an excerpt from the description of the ZOOXXI initiative posted on Decidim by its sponsors:

> *We want to leave behind the nineteenth-century model to adapt to new times...put aside the mercantilist and colonialist vision of the current zoo model, which reproduces exotic animals that are not in danger of extinction and will never be reintroduced into nature. If the initiative is successful, zoos will no longer be a mere exhibition space and become a conservation and protection space for long-term autochthonous fauna.*[10]

The ZOOXXI initiative represents precisely the kind of citizen involvement Barcelona hopes to encourage with its

Decidim platform. The city is also trying to spark citizen participation in an ongoing debate over the development of Las Ramblas, one of Barcelona's best-known destinations for tourists. The city wants to create citizen cooperative groups focusing on traffic, culture, community, and work. In addition to holding public workshops, the citizen cooperative groups will have the autonomy to create complementary programs, hold their own deliberative sessions, interview experts, organize street activities, and make inquiries independently. The city also provides meeting spaces and facilities for the citizen groups. Updates and information are posted on special pages of the city government website.[11]

With Decidim, the city walks a fine line between efficiency and anarchy. But Decidim equips Barcelona with the unique ability to crowdsource key processes of modern government. Instead of depending exclusively on politicians and consultants to chart its course, Barcelona also relies on the wisdom of crowds, one of humanity's oldest and most reliable sources of guidance.

Strengthening Social Ties

For some segments of the city's population, Barcelona takes a more direct approach to problem-solving. Vincles BCN is "a social innovation project designed to strengthen the social ties of elderly people who feel lonely and to improve their well-being with the aid of new technologies," according to the city's website.[12]

The program is provided by the Barcelona City Council Social Rights Area, which loans digital tablets to elderly residents. The tablets are preloaded with the Vincles app and data communication software, lowering barriers to usage by older citizens who aren't accustomed to using digital devices, finding local data networks, and uploading software.

Here are brief excerpts from the Vincles webpages:

> *The Vincles app is accessible and very intuitive, and it has been designed with elderly people in mind. It enables users to communicate and interact, through video calls and video or voice messages, with their family and friends as well as with elderly people belonging to the Vincles user group.*
>
> *The user's family and friends will have to download the Vincles app to their smartphone. It is available on Android and iOS. They will need Android 4.1 or a later version, or iOS 8 or a later version. To activate the app, the user will have to provide an access code to all those people who would like to be part of their family network.*[13]

The Vincles program was rolled out in five neighborhoods of the city. After testing and refinement, Vincles was extended to all neighborhoods in the city's Eixample and Sant Martí districts. The city's goal is to make the service available across all of Barcelona.

Meantime, Vincles is drawing praise from international organizations, such as Bloomberg Philanthropies, which sponsors the Mayor's Challenge, a competition that awards substantial prizes to innovative cities in the United States, Europe, and Latin America. Vincles competed against projects in 155 cities in the 2014 Mayor's Challenge and helped Barcelona win first prize, worth 5 million euros.[14]

Other finalists that year included Comoodle, a collaborative project in Kirklees, UK, that lets people share "stuff, space, and skills;" SynAthina, an online platform that breaks down administrative barriers in local government in Athens; the Biochar Project, an initiative launched in Stockholm to fight climate change; and Virtual Warsaw, a platform that enables people with visual impairments to navigate around the city more easily.[15]

Narrowing the Focus to Specific Segments

The Vincles initiative also illustrates the value of segmentation, a marketing technique that can be highly effective for addressing specific groups of users with similar needs.

Segmentation is the opposite of mass marketing. The core concept of segmentation is that different groups of people have different needs. Since most of us are consumers, we grasp that idea on an intuitive level. Almost every consumer brand you can think of uses varying degrees of segmentation. It's become a basic principle of modern business.

Governments have long resisted the idea of segmentation, for two main reasons:

1. Segmentation requires more work and continuous effort than mass marketing. Managing multiple segments of consumers is intrinsically more difficult than managing a mass market. With mass marketing, you develop a single strategy and you execute it. Mass marketing

worked fine in the 19th and 20th centuries, but its halcyon days are long gone. Segmentation, on the other hand, requires ongoing adjustment and refinement. Even though segmentation was developed before the advent of digital marketing and big data, it's a better fit for the 21st century.

2. Segmentation flies in the face of traditional government logic, which insists that every citizen is essentially the same person and should be treated the same way as every other citizen. Ask anyone with special needs or disabilities about their experiences with government and they'll regale you with stories about what it feels like to be treated the same as everyone else.

Smart-city initiatives must be explained and justified to citizens by local officials at neighborhood meetings and public events. They also must be marketed to citizens through social media and through traditional media channels, such as print, radio, television, and billboard advertising, using many of the same techniques normally used by businesses to market new products and services to potential customers.

Some government officials balk at the idea of marketing, but it's an indispensable part of rolling out smart-city initiatives. Every city should have in-house marketing capabilities and have a general sense of which modes of communication work best for interacting with its citizens.

If a city is promoting a new online system for paying taxes, then an email marketing campaign is probably the best option. If the city is promoting a new mobile app for keeping track of bus schedules, the best option might be placing posters and placards at bus stops.

The point is that you can't simply roll out a smart-city project and expect people to begin using it. Adoption is a slow process, and people need to see the value of using a new product or service, whether it's offered by a commercial enterprise like Apple or a city like Barcelona.

Works in Progress

In 2000, Barcelona created 22@District, a project for transforming a dilapidated section of the city into a hub for innovation. The government hoped the rejuvenated district would function as an urban seed crystal, eventually transforming Barcelona into a global innovation leader.

From the city's perspective, the district had everything necessary for success: a multinational pool of talented knowledge workers, numerous firms and businesses, and a strong sense of local community.

But years passed and the dream never quite jelled into reality. In 2007, the city commissioned a study of 22@District by the Imperial College Business School in London. Essentially, the city wanted to know why the project wasn't working out as planned.

The findings were sobering and instructive, according to a paper describing the study's results.[16] In brief, the study concluded that "one or even a small set of linked initiatives is not enough for success...a systemic approach is required." The study also suggested the city had incorrectly assumed that an abundance of "international human capital" would catalyze a major economic transformation. Additionally, the study cited the need for "proper measures" to integrate international workers with existing communities of firms and workers.

"Proactivity is needed in making connections between key players," writes Nick Leon, director of design at Imperial College Business School and Royal College of Art. "Cities that not only can *attract* but are proactive in *engaging and connecting* the international community with local firms and institutions are more likely to prosper in a highly competitive, knowledge-intensive, networked economy."[17]

It's the Journey, Not the Destination

Today, Barcelona is still refining and enhancing the 22@ District project. If you visit the Decidim website, you can see the latest ideas and proposals for the project. The evolution of 22@District brings to mind another famous but unfinished Barcelona project: Basílica i Temple Expiatori de la Sagrada Família.

Designed by Catalan architect Antoni Gaudí, La Sagrada Família is one of Barcelona's most beloved landmarks and tourist attractions. Every day, thousands of people visit the church and marvel at its spectacular design. Gaudí began working on the project in 1883. Construction is expected to finish in 2026, a full century after its designer's death.

Building a smart city is an exercise in both democracy and creativity. Both processes are invariably messy and unpredictable. Every smart city is a work in progress, much like La Sagrada Família. When Gaudí began designing the church, he built upside-down physical models to test his revolutionary ideas. The unorthodox approach made it easier for him to improvise and try out new designs.

There are no standard models or templates for building smart cities, because every city is different. The smart-cities movement is still young and the learning curve is steep. The smartest of the smart cities put their faith and trust in long-term iterative efforts. They patiently and painstakingly combine input and feedback from internal and external stakeholders and constituencies at all levels—bottom, top, and middle.

Smart cities like Barcelona and Tel Aviv offer several lessons:

1. Keep citizens in the loop.

2. Let their ideas percolate up.

3. Analyze mistakes and acknowledge them freely.

4. Use technology as a tool for bringing people together.

5. Crowdsource innovation.

6. Don't expect overnight success.

Endnotes

1. https://www.decidim.barcelona

2. https://decidim.org

3. https://github.com/decidim

4. https://meta.decidim.barcelona

5. https://www.ft.com/content/6d2fe2a8-722c-11e7-93ff-99f383b09ff9

6. http://ajuntament.barcelona.cat/digital/en

7. http://governobert.bcn.cat/en/noticia/decidimbarcelona-the-web-for-everyone-to-help-build-barcelona

8. https://www.theguardian.com/world/2016/oct/20/spanish-court-overturns-catalonia-bullfighting-ban

9. https://zooxxi.org/en

10. https://www.decidim.barcelona/processes/iniciativaciutadana zooxxi

11. http://ajuntament.barcelona.cat/lesrambles

12. http://ajuntament.barcelona.cat/vinclesbcn/en

13. http://ajuntament.barcelona.cat/vinclesbcn/en/how-does-it-work

14. http://ajuntament.barcelona.cat/vinclesbcn/en/bloomberg

15. http://mayorschallenge.bloomberg.org/bold-ideas

16. Nick Leon, "The 22@Barcelona Innovation District and the Internationalization of Barcelona Business," Innovation: Policy and Practice 10, no. 2–3 (2008). http://researchonline.rca.ac.uk/1098

17. http://researchonline.rca.ac.uk/1098

Chapter 8

Smart Nation

SITTING ON the Baltic Sea, Estonia is a land of forests, farmers, and folklore. It's also the birthplace of Skype. For decades, Estonia was a communist state. Today, it's a model of enlightened capitalism.

To outsiders, Estonia is a study in contradictions. Estonians enjoy solitude: Hiking alone in the woods is the national pastime. When they aren't wandering among the trees, Estonians are warm, friendly, and welcoming. They also put a high value on their individual privacy.

Estonia's distinct version of Nordic culture has created the perfect conditions for the world's first digital government.

"It's easier for me to tell you what I *cannot* do on my mobile phone than what I *can* do," says Martin Kõiva, a business executive from Tallinn, Estonia's capital. "Getting married, buying a home, and filing for divorce require your physical presence. Everything else you can do on your phone."

Estonians don't wait in lines to apply for licenses, pay taxes, or start new businesses. They don't have to show up in person to sign contracts, buy cars, register pets, or vote. Ninety-nine percent of government services are online.[1]

Kõiva recently arranged his grandmother's transfer from a hospital to a rehabilitation center. In most countries, moving a patient from one health care facility to another is a complicated and time-consuming process. In Estonia, it can be done on your mobile phone. "We really didn't have to do very much," he says. "All of her data was already in the national health care registry system. That's the part most people find interesting—there was no complexity. Everything was easy."

Estonia's e-government also makes doing business easier. Kõiva is the global head of customer support for Pipedrive, a company that makes sales software. Pipedrive is headquartered in Estonia and has offices in New York, London, and Lisbon. Kõiva spends part of his time working from the firm's Lisbon office, which gives him a firsthand view of the differences between traditional European bureaucracies and Estonia's e-government.

"E-government is a massive time-saver," he says. "For instance, in Estonia we almost never use paper contracts. When a contract is ready, you get an email notification and you use your digital signature to sign the contract. It doesn't matter who signs first or what order you sign in. When everyone has signed, you get another email. The whole process can be completed in minutes."

Faster contracting translates into faster cash flows, creating a feedback loop that accelerates the overall pace of business. "Dealing with countries where they still have a paper contracts and multiple layers of government bureaucracy can be frustrating," he says. "I occasionally misjudge the amount of time it takes to close deals in other countries because I'm accustomed to our system, which is fast and easy."

Tabula Rasa

What does it take to turn a national bureaucracy into a high-functioning e-government? It's not too often a country is given a clean slate from which to start. But for Estonia, that is exactly what happened.

There are several strands in the evolution of Estonia's e-government. During World War II, Estonia was occupied by the Soviets, then by the Nazis, and then again by the Soviets, who remained in control until the country regained its independence in 1991. By the time the country had regained its sovereignty, its economy was in ruins.

To rejoin the free world, Estonia needed to rebuild its institutions from the ground up, including its technology infrastructure.

Yet their experience with Soviet-style government left the Estonians with no urge to re-create a large bureaucracy.

"We had no legacy systems to maintain, so we were free to start from zero," Kõiva explains. "It was a great opportunity to choose our own destiny."

Naïve youths and country bumpkins are frequent archetypes in Estonian folktales. They face challenges or find opportunities; they are underestimated by opponents who are more sophisticated or powerful; they use their wits and tenacity to solve riddles or uncover hidden treasures; and more often than not, they emerge victorious.

In Estonian culture, common sense is a supreme virtue. "We admire people who are pragmatic and realistic," Kõiva explains. "We have a phrase in Estonian, *kaine talupojamõistus*, which translates roughly into 'healthy peasant reasoning.' It's our equivalent of 'common sense.' It embodies the idea of handling complex issues instinctively and without formal knowledge."

The combination of pragmatism and instinct led Estonia to develop an e-government in the 1990s. It was visionary and far ahead of its time. But Estonians didn't pursue a digital future because they thought it would be cool or trendy. They followed their common sense, which told them it would be better to expend their limited resources on servers and networks rather than grand buildings and government palaces.

Fortune Plays a Hand

In addition to common sense and pragmatism, good fortune played a role in Estonia's emergence as a leader in e-government.

Prior to serving as Estonia's president from 2006 to 2016, Toomas Hendrik Ilves had been the architect of Estonia's e-government system. Before that, he had been a prime mover of the country's program to put all of its schools online. He describes himself as a "geeky" evangelist for Estonia's strategy of "radical digitization."[2]

Ilves's path to leadership is a story in itself. He was born in Sweden to Estonian parents who later fled to the United States. He was raised in suburban New Jersey and learned to program in Basic in ninth grade. He has a bachelor's degree from Columbia University and master's degree from the University of Pennsylvania. He returned to Europe in the 1980s as a reporter for Radio Free Europe, where he met with underground dissidents who would become the core of the Estonian independence movement.

After Estonia regained its independence, Ilves served as ambassador to the United States, Canada, and Mexico simultaneously. He later became the nation's minister of foreign affairs. He also ran for political office in Estonia and became an observer member of the European Parliament. It would be hard to imagine Estonia's e-government initiative succeeding without Ilves's unusual combination of technical skill, life experience, and political clout.

Timing was another key factor in the development of Estonia's e-government. The collapse of the Soviet Union in 1991 and the emergence of Estonia as a free nation coincided with the rise of the Internet. Soon afterward, the development of the first web browser in 1993 transformed the internet from a science project into a worldwide social network. Had Estonia regained its independence even 10 years earlier, the story might be very different.

With the advent of the internet it became possible to envision digital systems capable of replacing physical systems on a grand scale. Led by visionaries such as Ilves, Estonia embarked on a brave experiment to reinvent government. Whether by intention or luck, Estonia also became the first smart nation.

X-Road

The backbone of Estonia's e-government is X-Road, a homegrown data exchange system that shuttles information instantly and securely between thousands of databases. Estonia estimates that X-Road saves more than 820 years of working time for the state and its citizens annually. More than 900 organizations and businesses in Estonia use X-Road daily.[3]

X-Road isn't a loosely connected network of servers. It's a highly secure platform for transmitting encrypted data with the precision and accuracy of a fine watch.

Estonia also has a strong national identity system underpinning its e-government infrastructure. Almost every Estonian has a secure digital ID, which is used for an endless variety of transactions, from riding public transit to signing official documents.

Estonia's e-government has no central or master database. Each agency or organization that's part of the system stores and administers its own data. Information about your taxes, traffic tickets, land transfers, education, voter registration, health care, and finances are stored in separate databases. Your information is encrypted. It cannot be shared without your knowledge and permission.

You can choose which health care providers see information from your other health care providers. You decide if you want your dentist to see information from your cardiologist, your dermatologist, or your psychotherapist.

Blockchain technology is embedded throughout the system, making it impossible to move data in or out without leaving a digital trace. All information is signed, time-stamped, and chained together to safeguard its integrity. All transactions are meticulously tracked and recorded. Data cannot be faked or manipulated, rendering it virtually incorruptible. When an agency, organization, or individual looks at your data, you are notified. There are penalties for accessing data improperly.

The goal of X-Road is making life easier at every level. For example, when a child is born, the hospital enters the information in its database, which is linked to the national population register. The information is shared automatically with the various government systems that will ensure that the child receives social benefits, such as health care and education.

It typically takes about three minutes to file a tax return in Estonia. The forms are prefilled; one click and you're done. Need to refill a prescription? You can do it online or on your phone.

From the Estonian perspective, X-Road fulfills the three basic requirements of a secure and practical data exchange platform:

1. Data must be easily accessible by authorized users and organizations.

2. Integrity of data must be maintained. No third party should be able to make any changes to data while it is in transit.

3. Data must remain confidential during its journey. It must be protected from the eyes of unauthorized parties.[4]

Building Trust through Practice

Unquestionably, Estonia's e-government system has benefited from a global phenomenon: People generally trust digital technology. We love our mobile phones, laptops, tablets, and PCs. The irony, of course, is that trust in digital tech is rising as trust in traditional government is falling. That's another reason why Estonia's experiment in digital government seems so smart: it's riding the zeitgeist.

Estonians today trust their system. But the trust wasn't automatic; it was earned. "You earn trust through practice and execution," says Linnar Viik, co-founder of the country's e-Governance Academy. "It's not just about being connected. You need to deliver value every day. We believe that a digital channel provides more accuracy, convenience, transparency, and trust. But we have to prove it."

The first part of the trust-building process is data owner-ship. "In Estonia, everyone owns their data. It's not owned by the government. This was a fundamental and very important concept. It means I can give my data to the government and I can take it back. I decide who can look at my data and who cannot look at my data," Viik says.

In a sense, every Estonian has an on/off switch controlling who has access to his or her data. As a result, Viik says, people don't spend a lot of time worrying about whether their data is secure or not. It also helps that Estonia hasn't experienced a large-scale data breach since launching its e-government.

The next part of building trust is total transparency. "I have an overview of what data the government has about me," Viik explains. "If I see the data is incorrect, I can trigger a correction."

The third part of the process is outright honesty. "If I'm driving and I get stopped by the police and they check the status of my driver's license and my car insurance, I will get a notification that my information was queried, along with the name of the police officer who stopped me," he says. If Estonians believe the police have misused their data, they can request assistance from an independent investigator who will help them find out why and how their data was used.

Viik acknowledges that broad trust in technology has proved helpful. But it's not a permanent free pass. "For most people, digital technology is a holistic experience," he notes. "Today, there is a sense of techno-optimism. Many people trust Google more than they trust their bank. Many people would rather find a diagnosis on the Web than talk to a doctor."

All of that could change overnight. People are fickle and easily swayed by headlines. Trust in popular social media networks is eroding, and Viik is rightfully concerned the tide could turn against digital government. "That's why we need long-term practices that build trust," he says.

A simple and successful practice has been making email a formal communication channel between citizens and government. Email is a good place to begin building trust in digital government, Viik says.

"The email address of your government cannot be a black hole that never responds to you," he explains. "Government needs to respond and confirm that it has received your message. You need to get a receipt saying, 'Yes, we got your message and it's in our pipeline.' The receipt must be generated immediately. Then it has real impact. The citizen thinks, 'This is much better than sending a letter or standing in line. It's the middle of the night, I'm sitting in front of my computer, I send an email and *poof,* my request is already being processed.'"

Once Only

In addition to promising security and efficiency, Estonia's e-government engenders trust in numerous subtle ways. For instance, it's a given that Estonians enter their personal information only once. Estonians don't spend lots of time filling out forms because most forms are prefilled.

You aren't continually asked or required to re-enter your personal information (name, date of birth, employment status, email address, phone number, home address, etc.) when applying for loans, renewing your passport, or registering your child for kindergarten.

You enter your secure ID and the system does the rest, automatically populating forms with your personal data. It would be unusual for an organization or agency to require you to fill out a form manually. Since most transactions are handled machine to machine, your personal data is rarely seen by another human being.

The "once only" policy sends a clear signal to Estonians. It says, "Your government respects your time and your privacy."

Safeguarding privacy, something Estonians hold very dear, is front and center in the e-government. As mentioned earlier, Estonia hasn't been part of a major security breach, but that doesn't mean there haven't been efforts.

Turning an Attack into a Challenge

In 2007, Estonia was the target of a distributed denial of service (DDoS) attack that temporarily brought its digital society to a standstill. The attack, thought by many to have been launched by Russia, did not penetrate the security of the Estonian cybersystems—it merely froze them.

But the blatantly hostile maneuver left an indelible mark—not just on Estonia, but on the rest of Europe as well. In many ways, it demonstrated the strength and resiliency of Estonian digital infrastructure. It proved that Estonia could withstand the assault of a well-armed foe. It also prompted NATO to establish its Cooperative Cyber Security Defence Centre of Excellence in the Estonian capital.[5]

In a strange way, the cyberattack became a stealth endorsement for Estonian technology. Everyone in the tech industry knew that the Estonians had been attacked by a superior force and had survived largely unscathed. It's a great story that combines the plot twists of a modern techno-thriller with the sad truth that Russia and Estonia have been battling each other sporadically for roughly 10 centuries.

It also put Estonia on the alert. The country's digital systems are now mirrored in secure backup sites abroad. If necessary, Estonia's e-government can be managed from anywhere in the world.

But most Estonians don't think about their e-government in geopolitical terms. They're happy it works for them. It gets the job done. And the e-government isn't just about helping citizens manage their personal and professional lives more effectively. It also has a system for keeping those who want to be better informed about what's going on within the country.

In the Know

The e-government system also keeps Estonians abreast of what's happening in their "traditional" government. If you're interested in a particular topic—say, national defense or immigration—you can sign up for alerts to find out when government officials will be debating it.

"When the national cabinet meets, its agenda is posted online one week before the meeting," Viik says. "I can see everything the cabinet will discuss, including supporting materials. So if there are topics I follow—such as forestry and education—I'll know beforehand. When the cabinet makes a decision, I will be informed. All of that increases transparency."

Estonians don't see their government as Big Brother. Orwell's omniscient dictator could peer into every living room while his hapless subjects suffered in ignorance. Many Estonians have read *1984* and most Estonians are old enough to remember living under harsh Soviet rule. Would they willingly choose to relive those dark days? It seems unlikely.

Estonia's e-government reflects the national character. It's a practical tool, designed primarily to save time and money while still respecting personal privacy.

"We believe that the state must be invisible in daily affairs, but always immediately accessible when needed. Time is a valuable resource for the state and for every single citizen. Spending time on bureaucracy reduces the state's competitiveness and people's quality of life," writes Heiko Vainsalu, a former IT architect at the Estonian Information System Authority.[6]

The Shape of Things to Come

Estonia's successful experiment with e-government has not gone unnoticed. Elements of its systems are gradually spreading to other countries. Estonia has exported e-government solutions, including X-Road, to more than 130 countries, including Finland, Oman, Ukraine, the Faroe Islands, Macedonia, Namibia, Tunisia, Kyrgyzstan, and India, according to Vainsalu.

Cross-border access to systems and data creates new opportunities. If you've ever run out of a prescription medication in a foreign country, you know how difficult it can be to replace it. X-Road will soon give Estonians and Finns the choice of picking up their pharmacy prescriptions in Estonia or Finland. "A lot of Estonians work in Finland and a lot of Finns visit Estonia for business and holidays," says Hannes Astok, deputy director for strategy and development at the Estonian e-Governance Academy.

To outsiders, the most impressive piece of Estonia's e-government is the trust Estonians have placed in it. Estonia is a small country—only 1.4 million people—and even total strangers feel as though they know each other. That sense of kinship engenders levels of trust that would be hard to replicate in larger nations. "We trust our government officials because we often know them personally," explains Martin Kõiva.

It would be easy to dismiss Estonia's e-government as something only suited to a small Nordic country. Although it's a sovereign nation, its population is that of a medium-size city. But it faces many of the same challenges confronting cities—limited resources, an aging workforce, competition from rivals, and uncertain economic prospects.

There's still quite a bit we can learn from Estonia, even if some of its systems would be hard to replicate elsewhere. Pioneering initiatives, such as X-Road in Estonia, DigiTel in Tel Aviv, and Decidim in Barcelona, offer tantalizing glimpses into the future. They aren't perfect, but they're the shape of things to come.

Endnotes

1. https://e-estonia.com/solutions/interoperability-services/x-road

2. https://www.forbes.com/forbes/welcome/?toURL=https://www.forbes.com/sites/peterhigh/2018/04/23/an-interview-with-the-architect-of-the-most-digitally-savvy-country-on-earth/&refURL=&referrer=#5b5faf3d1dc1

3. https://e-estonia.com/how-save-annually-820-years-of-work

4. https://www.youtube.com/watch?v=9PaHinkJlvA

5. https://ccdcoe.org

6. https://e-estonia.com/how-save-annually-820-years-of-work

Chapter 9

Paint a Bull's-Eye on Them

"Pride goeth before destruction, and an haughty spirit before a fall."

—Proverbs 16:18 (King James Version)

THAT SMART CITY you're so proud of? That city you worked so hard to design, build, maintain, and keep safe? It's a big, juicy target for cyberattackers.

You think the cybersecurity breaches at Target, Equifax, Anthem, and JPMorgan Chase & Co. were bad?[1] Those breaches will seem piddling compared with what will happen to smart cities. Worried about WannaCry, MyDoom, Slammer, Stuxnet, and the Mirai botnet?[2] We'll look back on those with nostalgia after a cyberattack takes down an entire smart city.

"A smart city will be under constant attack," says Chris Moschovitis, a cybersecurity expert in New York. "You will need to defend your city and its assets against individuals and organizations that will attempt to exploit weaknesses in your cybersystems."

Cybercrime will occur at all levels of the smart city. Today, cities worry about fare cheaters jumping over turnstiles in subway stations. Tomorrow, the fare cheaters won't bother to jump because they'll know how to override the turnstile's security controls.

Every department in the city will have its own set of assets, threats, and risk registers.[3] Each department will have its own set of mission-critical systems and vulnerabilities. The complexities will be daunting. The consequences of failure will range from trivial to catastrophic. Providing cybersecurity for a smart city will not be an easy task. There will be no simple solutions. Smart cities will need to maintain a continual state of vigilance and readiness against cyberattacks.

Pete Herzog, a cybersecurity consultant based in Spain, says smart cities should prepare for three kinds of attackers: the bored, the desperate, and the villainous.

The Bored

"The bored are simply people who see an opportunity and grab it," Herzog says. "They may not have master skills to hack the systems but they have time to learn. The best way to deal with them is to know your networks, know how your systems interoperate with people, and monitor your systems for activity that is off the baseline or unusual."

The Desperate

The desperate include people who need services offered by a smart city, yet who are prevented from using those services for various reasons. For example, a smart city might decide to put some of its services off-limits to felons, sex offenders, or minors. Some people will encounter language barriers or accessibility issues when they try to use smart-city services. Since many city services might be available only through smart phones, some people who need city services and who don't own smart phones will find workarounds enabling them to use the services illegally.

"The desperate will find ways to do what they need to do. They will break laws and hack into systems to obtain services. They will become costly public nuisances. Smart cities will have to anticipate this and make sure they provide ways of accommodating people who cannot access smart services legally or easily," Herzog says. "There will be lots of people who want to use smart services and who will be locked out for one reason or another. Smart cities will need to look beyond the needs of the simple majority and develop systems that everyone can use."

The Villainous

The villainous include nation-states, terrorist organizations, and crime syndicates. Sometimes a villain will be a combination of all three. "These are people with unlimited resources. Their goal is causing chaos and destruction. They sow fear and anxiety. They have the time and the resources to attack. They will keep trying and they will be a constant threat," Herzog says.

Technology by itself will not protect smart cities from the concerted efforts of spies, terrorists, and criminals. Neither will *defense in depth*, which requires multiple layers of cybersecurity controls. Cybersecurity vendors love defense-in-depth strategies because they are expensive to build and maintain. "First, you build a castle to protect your data. Then you build another castle inside the first castle. And then you build another castle inside that one. And by the way, each castle has a moat with its own crocodiles," Moschovitis says.

He's kidding, or course, although he raises two excellent points:

1. Attackers won't be the only ones targeting smart cities. Cybersecurity vendors will see them as prospective customers for their latest, greatest products and services.

2. Products and services alone won't stop cyberattacks. Coping successfully with cyberattacks will require orchestrated efforts by broad coalitions of stakeholders.

"Cities will need good processes for working with state, federal, and international law enforcement organizations. Cities will need to create and staff teams of responders, investigators, and lawyers to deal with cybercrime," Herzog says.

Citizens at every level will need to develop "keener senses of situational awareness" and know where to turn for help when they suspect that a cyberattack has occurred, he says.

Concepts such as "guardianship" and "eyes on the street" will extend into cyberspace. In New York City, everyone knows the phrase, "If you see something, say something." After the attacks on Sept. 11, 2001, it became a motto. For many New Yorkers, it's become a habit. If you see a strange package lying on the floor of Grand Central Station, you tell a cop. Better to be safe than sorry. Eventually, we'll have similar phrases reminding people to be watchful for cyberthreats.

Smart cities will also deploy continuous surveillance systems to monitor public spaces in real time for potentially dangerous activities. Some of the data collected by those systems will be stored for future analysis. The data must be stored securely, however, to prevent cybercriminals from stealing it and selling it on the dark net to blackmailers, extortionists, burglars, and thieves.

Small Disruptions Can Have Large Consequences

Dale Meyerrose, a retired US Air Force major general and former CIO for the US intelligence community, frames the challenges in simple terms. "Cybersecurity is something you do, not something you buy," Meyerrose says. "It's all about people and their behavior. Edward Snowden downloaded thousands of intelligence files and then walked out the door. It's amazing how we can get the technology parts right and the people parts wrong."

Since it's easier to buy new technology than it is to change the behavior of people, the temptation to rely on technology is virtually irresistible. But smart cities that become overly reliant on technology to handle cybersecurity will inevitably find themselves unprepared to cope with the harsh realities of cyberspace.

"Even if you decide to rely on technology, there's no one-size-fits-all solution. Every city has a different mix of services and assets, which means that every city will need to customize its approach to cybersecurity," Meyerrose says. "The rule of thumb is that 80 percent of your strategy will be similar to what every other city is doing, but 20 percent will be particular to your city. So you can't simply copy and paste another city's strategy."

Meyerrose dispels the notion that a cyberattack could paralyze a city. Most cities operate hundreds of systems and only a handful of those systems actually communicate with each other. Even the most advanced smart cities don't have fully interoperable systems. From Meyerrose's perspective, the lack of full interoperability works in a city's favor.

"A highly skilled evildoer might be able to take down one or two systems, but the likelihood of a cyberattack taking down a whole city is very small," he says.

But he's not saying that cybersecurity doesn't matter. "Even a small disruption in a vital city service could have a large consequence," Meyerrose says. "Cities are densely populated, and panic can spread easily. Attackers know that, and they will use a city's density as a weapon against it."

Sowing seeds of mistrust will become a common ploy of cyberattackers targeting smart cities. Instead of destroying property, they will focus on creating a steady stream of irritations and inconveniences designed to gradually wear down citizens, lower their morale, and erode their trust in social institutions.

In "Monsters on Maple Street," a classic episode of *The Twilight Zone*, residents of a small town are incited to violence against each other by alien invaders who randomly disrupt the town's electricity. Rod Serling, the show's creator, foresaw the tactics of 21st-century cyberwarfare.

"The primary threats to a smart city will be the people in the city," Meyerrose says. "Cyberattackers will take the path of least resistance. They're not going to attack your strongest defensive positions—they'll find the weak spots. They'll come in through cracks and holes."

That means they'll probably use phishing tactics to place malware on servers and in systems. Or they'll look for vulnerabilities and launch DDoS attacks. In March 2018, GitHub, the repository in which many software developers store their projects, was taken offline by the largest DDoS attack in history.[4] Because GitHub is run by and for software developers, the site was only down for 10 minutes. For people outside of geek culture, that idea that GitHub could be taken down might seem like no big deal. But for programmers and developers, it was the equivalent of Goldfinger's raid on Fort Knox. If GitHub can go down, nothing is safe in cyberspace.

Managing cybersecurity in urban areas will be a major challenge of our time, Meyerrose predicts. As more people move to cities, the cities themselves will become geopolitical players. Cities with strong cybersecurity will contribute to geopolitical stability; cities with poor security will contribute to instability.

For example, if you wanted to attack a city with strong cyber defenses, you might start by attacking and destabilizing weaker cities near your primary target. Your goal would be creating a zone of instability around the primary target, making an attack against it more likely to succeed.

This isn't science fiction; cyberwarfare tactics have already been used to weaken or destabilize regimes in Europe, Asia, and the Middle East. If you live in the United States, it's difficult to escape daily reports on cable news stations about alleged Russian meddling in the 2016 presidential election. It would be hard to find a sizable country without cyberwarfare capabilities. China's military has identified cyberspace as one of its four critical security domains (the other domains are sea, space, and nuclear).[5]

Data in Motion

A smart city is a system composed of many systems. Each subsidiary system, from the smallest to the largest, is an integration of sensors, applications, networks, and data centers.

The city has sensors and applications monitoring traffic, air quality, water treatment, mass transit, emergency communications, light, and power. All of those sensors and apps send data across networks to data centers operated by the city and its vendors.

Some of the data is sent to data centers that are physically located within the city and some is sent into the cloud. Data that is sent into the cloud can wind up in data centers anywhere in the world, from Reykjavík to St. Petersburg.[6]

A smart city encrypts its data, so bad guys can't read it, even if they manage to steal it. What kind of data is worth stealing? You would be surprised. A brief cruise through the dark net[7] reveals a panoply of stolen data for sale. Cybercrime is a highly creative business and there's a buyer for everything: medical records, union contracts, payrolls, parking tickets, financial statements, divorce filings, hospital admissions, reservoir levels, and truancy rates.

Every bit of information generated by the city's thousands of systems must be encrypted, from the faintest signals sent by tiny sensors in the doors of subway cars to emergency responder calls—all of that information must be encrypted before it's sent over a network.

But data encryption is only one of many steps the city takes to defend itself. The city is a system of systems, and each system has a life cycle. Cybersecurity controls (detective, preventive, mediating, and compensating) must be applied throughout the life cycle of each system.

"The systems in a smart city are not static," Moschovitis says. "They are in a state of continuous flux. Your cybersecurity controls have to keep pace with those changes or they will quickly become useless."

For practical purposes, that means every system needs a thorough cybersecurity review. The city must commit itself to maintaining strict cybersecurity discipline across multiple systems, each with its own life cycle.

"It's especially important when lives are at stake," he says. "When your main concern is protecting data, you can use a simple risk assessment model called C-I-A, which stands for confidentiality, integrity, and availability. But since smart cities are all about people, you have to expand your model to include safety. Now your model is C-I-A + S, because if hackers start messing with traffic lights or subway trains, people can get hurt or even killed."

People Are Worth More Than Data

Safety throws a wrench into the traditional method of determining how much to spend protecting cyber assets. For years, the rule of thumb was simple: never spend more to protect an asset than the asset is worth.

When safety is added to the equation, the rule of thumb goes out the window. For example, let's say the sensor in the subway car door costs $3. Does that mean you won't spend more than $3 protecting it, even when you know that if it fails, a rider might be hurt?

If a subway car door closes on a rider's hand or foot, the cost of the injury will far exceed the cost of the sensor in the door. If the injured rider decides to sue the city, the cost will be even higher.

Smart cities will have to invent new ways of modeling risk, valuing assets, and setting spending priorities. If the emergency braking system in a smart elevator is hacked and the elevator plunges 100 floors before hitting the ground, the first thought in everyone's mind won't be the cost of the elevator.

That said, it's possible to imagine situations in which landlords and property owners apply old-school thinking to their risk-management calculations and fail to protect their assets adequately from cyberattacks. Then it's up to the city to set standards for cybersecurity and to enforce those standards.

Maintaining cybersecurity in a smart city will be a shared responsibility; every organization will need to follow the same basic rule book. It would be hard to imagine a smart city in which the public and private sectors had radically different sets of rules governing their approaches to cybersecurity.

Nevertheless, some cities will set rules that are overly restrictive and some will set rules that are overly lax. Undoubtedly, politics will be a factor in determining how strictly or how loosely the rules are devised and enforced. Hopefully, most cities will find a middle ground between the extremes and will develop cybersecurity strategies that protect people while simultaneously safeguarding their privacy and property rights.

Cybersecurity by Design

Many smart cities will adopt a strategy known as *security by design*,[8] in which security principles are carefully and conscientiously applied to every part of every system and to all transactions at all levels in all systems. Security by design assumes that systems will be compromised and that data will be lost or stolen. Instead of building walls *around* data, devices, and processes, it embeds security *into* them.

It's also a mind-set that embodies a constant state of awareness. "You focus on securing processes instead of racing around and reacting to threats," Herzog says. "Since you can't possibly know every weakness, it doesn't make sense to focus all of your security efforts on managing vulnerabilities."

Many attacks can be thwarted by simply separating systems and processes. "Terminating SSL (Secure Sockets Layer) connections in front of web servers prevents a whole security layer from being abused by attackers trying to break into those web servers," he says. "Prohibiting desktops and laptops from sharing data with each other on the intranet prevents the spread of malware. Closing ports and services on a network will greatly reduce attacks."

Preparation and management also play important roles in deterring cyberattackers. "Money doesn't buy security," says Herzog. "Planning and effort are required. For instance, it's a good practice to give workers more breaks later in the day when they're getting tired and they're more likely to be fooled by an attacker's tricks. Taking breaks clears your mind and makes you less susceptible to the ploys and lures used by attackers."

Early in his career, Herzog believed that merely talking about cybercrime would be enough to encourage people to behave more carefully. "I was so naïve," he recalls. "People already know that criminals operate in cyberspace. They get that. But the number of ways an attack can play out is nearly infinite, so telling people about dramatic attacks that happened in the past won't really help them prepare for future attacks."

Training, education, and periodic reminders are necessary. "As a smart-city manager or director, you need to remind your people not to click on links that seem unfamiliar or suspicious," he says. "Phishing remains an enormous problem, so remind people not to click on links without first examining them carefully. And that includes anything sent to them via Facebook, Twitter, LinkedIn, Instagram, Snapchat, or other forms of social media."

Sysadmins (system administrators) will need additional situational awareness training, since they are absolutely essential to the process of defending a smart city against cyberattacks. "There's no use putting locks on doors if people leave them open," says Herzog.

Convincing sysadmins to spend *more* time on cybersecurity (which they see as their secondary role) and *less* time on keeping systems running efficiently (which they see as their primary role) won't be easy.

"You've got to show everyone with administrative access to a system how it can be attacked and compromised. Show them how they can be manipulated and fooled by attackers. Show them how changes in their work environment will prevent them from being caught off guard and will minimize the chances of an attack being successful," Herzog says. "After they understand, they will become much more effective defenders against security threats."

The Smart-City CISO

Smart cities will acknowledge and understand the risks posed by cyber vulnerabilities. They will develop strategies for deterring cyberattacks, reducing risks, and foiling attackers. They will learn how to recover quickly from attacks, even after the attackers have crippled or compromised vital assets.

Every smart city will need a chief information security officer (CISO). The CISO is not the same as the CIO. In fact, the two roles are often in conflict.

In a smart city, the CIO creates value for citizens by choosing, deploying, and maintaining the best and most appropriate technologies. The CIO is always on the lookout out for cool and innovative tech that will make the lives of city residents easier and more enjoyable. The CIO goes home at night and sleeps peacefully.

The CISO, on the other hand, worries every minute of every day, because hackers and cybercriminals work around the clock, seven days a week. While the CIO dreams of a brighter future enabled by technology, the CISO foresees danger in every new application and device the city brings into its technology portfolio.

The CISO imagines everything that can possibly go wrong. The CISO looks around corners and figures out how to respond when hackers steal critical data or cybercriminals shut down vital public systems.

The CIO *creates* value and the CISO *protects* value. That puts them at odds. They might be friendly on a social level, yet they will eye each other warily. From the CISO's perspective, each new piece of tech expands the attack surface for bad guys and each new system opens up new attack vectors. The CISO thinks the CIO is an incurable optimist and the CIO thinks to CISO is a hopeless paranoid.

Hierarchies and Networks

The CISO is responsible for ensuring that every department in the city follows a set of formal cybersecurity practices. Ideally, each department will be audited at periodic intervals to make certain they're following the city's rules for cybersecurity. The auditors will check the effectiveness of each department's cyber controls and perform penetration tests to uncover vulnerabilities in its cybersystems.

"Auditors keep everybody honest," Moschovitis says. "But they'll need specific cybersecurity skills to be effective. People with those skills are few and far between. There is a tremendous shortage of experienced cyber auditors and they're expensive to hire."

Hiring inexperienced auditors would be less expensive, yet also less effective. "You cannot simply hand someone a checklist and expect them to make the city secure against cyberattackers," he says. "Cybersecurity is not a rote exercise; the minute you start using a checklist, you've failed because the bad guys will get a hold of your checklist and use it against you."

The CISO also will make sure that change-management procedures are followed properly when systems are replaced or upgraded. "When a department replaces system A with system B, it needs to follow established change-management protocols," Moschovitis explains. "You cannot simply swap systems, especially when those systems are connected to other systems all over the city. Ineffective change management can open huge security holes in complex systems."

A Universe of Connected People and Devices

In large cities, each department will have its own CISO. In addition to watching over cybersecurity in his or her functional domain, the departmental CISO will act as a deputy to the city CISO.

The city CISO and the deputy CISOs will form both a hierarchy and a network, reflecting the nature of the city itself. In a smart city, there are no stand-alone devices, applications, or systems. Everything is connected and to some degree, interdependent.

For example, the ticket machines at the train station might seem like stand-alone devices, but they're connected to the city's transit, financial, and electrical systems. Since the ticket machines accept credit cards in addition to cash, they're also connected to the privately owned and operated financial systems that process credit card payments.

Like the ticket machines, the small sensors in the subway that detect the approach of trains are both stand-alone devices and nodes in a network. Essentially, every device and application plays a dual role. It's an interesting phenomenon and a fundamental aspect of the Internet of Things (IoT). Several years ago, the experts at the National Institute of Standards and Technology predicted that smart cities would be the "best use case for the Internet of Things."

They were right. Smart cities are subsets of the IoT, which means they are also subsets of the Internet. That's more than a clever observation. It's a scary fact. The Internet has many wonderful qualities; security isn't one of them.

As metaphorical children of the IoT and grandchildren of the Internet, smart cities possess the strengths and weaknesses of their progenitors. They are broadly useful and usable. They are painfully difficult to secure. Security is to smart cities what kryptonite is to Superman.

Just as Superman's fear of kryptonite doesn't stop him from flying around and doing good deeds, smart cities must overcome their fear of cybercrime. We're not suggesting that cities should ignore the threat of cybercrime; we're saying that cities should acknowledge it and do everything in their power to fight it.

"In cybersecurity, there's always a push-pull between the fear of the inevitable and the art of the possible," Meyerrose says. "It's important not to allow your fear to prevent you from accomplishing what's possible. Your security won't be perfect, and that's all right. Imagine you're with a bunch of people being chased by a bear. You don't have to outrun the bear. You just have to outrun the slowest person in the bunch."

Endnotes

1. https://www.csoonline.com/article/2130877/data-breach/the-biggest-data-breaches-of-the-21st-century.html

2. https://uk.norton.com/norton-blog/2016/02/the_8_most_famousco.html

3. https://www.cio.com.au/article/401244/how_create_risk_register

4. http://www.zdnet.com/article/new-world-record-ddos-attack-hits-1-7tbps-days-after-landmark-github-outage

5. Department of Defense Annual Report to Congress, Military and Security Developments Involving the People's Republic of China 2017

https://www.defense.gov/Portals/1/Documents/pubs/
2017_China_Military_Power_Report.PDF

6. http://blackswanzine.com/2009/10/26/data-center-top-10-
countries-to-build-a-data-center

7. http://www.oreilly.com/webops-perf/free/patrolling-the-dark-
net.csp

8. https://www.owasp.org/index.php/Security_by_Design_
Principles

Chapter 10

Finding a Balance

DATA AND data science will play enormous roles in smart cities. A decade ago, it was common for writers to describe data as "the new oil." In retrospect, that comparison was far too limited. Data is more like the new money. If you think we're exaggerating, just look at the cryptocurrency markets.

Cryptocurrencies such as Bitcoin, Etherium, Ripple, Dash, Monero, and Steem are essentially created from data. They have no physical counterparts; they exist only within the realm of data science.

People have been arguing for centuries about the nature of money. Some say "The love of money is the root of all evil," and others say, "Money makes the world go round." Similarly conflicting sentiments are expressed about data.

If you're a cancer patient waiting for treatment, data might guide your physicians to the best combination of therapies.

If you're a convicted felon awaiting sentencing, data might add another year to your prison term.

Throughout this book, we have taken an optimistic view of data and data science. We're not unaware of the potential ways in which data can be misused. Even so, we're sticking to our basic belief that when it's used wisely, data is a force for good. That's why we've filled this book with information and examples demonstrating the value of data and data science within the context of smart cities.

Data for Good

"Smart cities are giant social hubs where people live healthy lives, get to work on time, and don't worry about getting hit by cars as they cross the street," says Jake Porway, founder and executive director of DataKind, a nonprofit that connects socially minded data scientists with organizations working to resolve complex humanitarian issues.

"For us, 'data for good' means using cutting-edge data science techniques like AI and machine learning to solve social problems and really help people," Porway says.

With data science, smart cities can determine which intersections are most dangerous and which remedies are most likely to reduce accidents; which homes need smoke alarms; which schools require monitoring for potential violence; which sources of water are most likely to contain contaminants; which parks are most used and need extra maintenance; and which neighborhoods would most likely benefit from additional police patrols at night.

"We see data science and data scientists playing major roles in smart cities," Porway says. "Data science gives you greater visibility into what's happening and reveals hidden patterns that can help cities make better decisions about allocating resources."

Even though data scientists are highly sought after—and highly compensated—many of them want to use their skills to help humanity, Porway says. What they need most are opportunities to apply their skills and experience to solving the kinds of social challenges that typically arise in cities.

"Most of the data scientists I know would rather help other people than spend their careers optimizing search-engine marketing programs," Porway says. "They represent a huge resource that smart cities can tap into."

With support from Microsoft, DataKind has partnered with Vision Zero to reduce traffic fatalities, design safer streets, and improve sidewalks in New York, Seattle, and New Orleans. "We needed information at a very granular level ... we needed to know where the cars were on a block-by-block basis. Data and predictive analytics allowed us to understand when and where accidents were happening," Porway says.

The key to success was learning how to partner effectively with multiple organizations and stakeholders. "We worked with police agencies, health departments, transportation authorities, private companies, and nonprofits," Porway says. One of the main lessons, he says, is "smart-city projects involve lots of cross-sector collaboration."

Location, Location, Location

In Chapter 2, we touched briefly on geographic information systems (GISs) and their role in helping cities make the best use of their data. In this chapter, we'll take a deeper dive into GISs and explain why GISs are an essential part of smart-city ecosystems.

"Everything in a city functions in the context of location," says Amen Ra Mashariki, head of urban analytics at Esri, a global supplier of mapping software and spatial analytics. "That means all a city's crucial data can and should be connected to specific places. But the information in its raw form isn't always available with a geographic component."

City budget data, for example, is immeasurably more valuable when it's connected to a location. In other words, it's not enough to know how much money is being spent—you also have to know *where* it's being spent.

"If you know where the city is spending money, you can get a more precise picture," Mashariki explains. "This, in turn, lets planners be more conscious about budget allocation being equitable—going to the places that need it most. So, with GIS, you can not only see where the need for investment is greatest, but you can also track the success of that spending after it has been applied."

Prior to joining Esri, Mashariki was New York City's chief analytics officer. His first-hand knowledge of city operations and his understanding of data science give him a unique perspective. He doesn't believe any city can be genuinely smart without GIS capabilities.

"Without the spatial understanding that GIS brings, cities simply can't have the kind of precision necessary to make informed decisions," he says." Location intelligence allows planners and citizens to see where issues are occurring and where to target the appropriate solutions."

During the summer of 2015, Mashariki recalls, there was an outbreak of Legionnaire's disease that left seven people dead and 86 infected in the South Bronx. "City officials managed to identify the source of the infection—cooling towers filled with the disease-causing bacteria—and used GIS to place the event in a *where* and *when* context," he explains.

Once MODA (Mayor's Office of Data Analytics) understood where the infection originated and how far it had spread, the New York City Council voted unanimously to pass a strict regulation requiring all cooling towers to be registered, tested, cleaned, and sterilized if they were found to contain *Legionella* bacteria.[1]

Another case involved landlords of rent-stabilized units who were allegedly harassing low-income tenants in an effort to get them to move. "One method they used was to start lengthy and complex construction to improve buildings, making them effectively uninhabitable, forcing tenants out, and then leasing at a higher rent," Mashariki explains.

But it was difficult to discern which landlords were harassing tenants and which were performing legitimate construction projects. "So MODA built a harassment timeline model that took several datasets into account and layered them," Mashariki says. The city also used a GIS to identify rent-stabilized buildings where harassment was likely.

MODA's model helped the city determine 1,000 possible locations where harassment was occurring. "Sixteen buildings were investigated," Mashariki says, leading to several high-profile arrests.

"You don't have to be a scientist to benefit from location intelligence data," he says. "When you see a map enriched with data, it places vital information in a geographic context...and you can make your own informed decisions. In that way, GIS really is democratization of knowledge."

Whenever there's a catastrophe, Mashariki says, response teams have the same question: *Where has this happened before?* "Maps have a unique ability to tell the story," he says, through presenting complex data in a common format that most people can easily understand.

Mashariki's examples demonstrate how smart cities leverage the intrinsic value of data to help citizens and make their lives better. Not all instances of data collection and analysis are as clearly beneficial. In the next section, we'll look at some of the questions raised by the use of data that smart cities routinely collect and analyze.

Hard Questions

The relationship between smart cities and data is unavoidable. You can't have one without the other. Pretending otherwise would be worse than foolish—it would be dangerous. You cannot manage large complex systems without data. Everything would eventually grind to a halt.

Continuous data collection and monitoring will be standard features of smart cities. Anything that interacts in any meaningful way with anything else will be tracked and monitored. It's not a matter of choice—the systems and processes that enable smart cities to operate won't work unless they're continually monitored, analyzed, and optimized. For smart cities, standing still is not an option. When you're dealing with systems of systems, the goal is continuous refinement, not maintaining the status quo.

Most of us are okay with the idea of collecting data from machines and systems. Smart cities will also gather data about people. In some situations, that will make us uncomfortable.

It would be naïve to believe that smart cities won't collect data about residents, commuters, and visitors as they walk on streets, use mass transit, ride in elevators, enter and leave buildings, attend public events, buy groceries, bring their children to school, meet with friends, and engage in hundreds of routine activities over the course of an average day.

Data collection on a massive scale raises thousands of questions. Here's an easy one: *Will smart cities collect data?* The answer is yes.

Other questions will be considerably more difficult to answer. Here's a small sample of hard questions cities will face as they gain access to greater amounts of data:

What will cities do with the data they collect?

Who determines what cities can do with the data they collect?

Who sets the limits on what kinds of data can and cannot be collected?

Who can see the data?

Who can use the data?

Who owns the data?

Who is responsible for the quality of the data?

Who is responsible for safeguarding the data?

Who is responsible if the data is leaked or stolen?

Is the data erased after a set period of time, or is it kept forever?

It's not just the data itself that raises legions of difficult questions. The data is fed into algorithms designed to generate information that can be used to make decisions about everything from turning on streetlights to setting bail for accused felons.

Algorithms are mathematical tools for solving problems. Unlike familiar equations such as $E = mc^2$ and $a^2 + b^2 = c^2$, which represent eternal truths, algorithms age over time. They need continual tuning and rewriting. Sometimes, they need to be scrapped and redone from scratch. You can't simply write an algorithm, pour data into it, and walk away.

As citizens, we need to begin asking tougher questions about algorithms: Who writes them? Who determines if they are effective? Who reviews them for fairness? Who determines whether they are helping or hurting people? If you believe you have been wronged by an algorithm, who will help you fight back?

Algorithmic Bias

Inevitably, algorithms reflect the biases of their creators. In *Weapons of Math Destruction*, former Wall Street quant Cathy O'Neil provides numerous examples of algorithms creating more unfairness and exacerbating existing inequalities in areas ranging from credit scores to jail sentences.

O'Neil is a data scientist, and she understands the value of good data. She is also keenly aware of the risks of applying data science haphazardly. In her book, she relates a harrowing story about a school district that used algorithms to rank the performance of teachers and ended up firing some of its best teachers.

The problem with algorithms is that while they *seem* scientific, they're really nothing more than digital tools. In most of our legal jurisdictions, human beings are held to far higher standards than algorithms, which is a disturbing thought when you consider their growing power over us. O'Neil sums up the issue neatly in her description of the school system that used algorithms to determine which teachers to fire:

> *An algorithm processes a slew of statistics and comes up with a probability that a certain person might be a bad hire, a risky borrower, a terrorist, or a miserable teacher. That probability is distilled into a score, which can turn someone's life upside down.*

Yet when the victim of a bad algorithm tries to appeal its verdict, the human is expected to present ironclad evidence that the algorithm is wrong. Unless you're a highly skilled data scientist, however, you're unlikely to win a fight against a flawed algorithm.

As algorithms play larger roles in our lives, their inherent limitations are becoming more obvious. Despite the risks posed by algorithms, there's no going back. For many of the same reasons we're not going to stop using computers, we're not going to stop using algorithms.

In fact, we're going to use them more and more. Smart cities don't merely need lots of computational power to run smoothly—they need artificial intelligence. AI programs essentially teach themselves how to analyze data and write algorithms, which is all well and good until something goes wrong. When your car breaks down, you can raise the hood and look at the engine to see if there's a broken radiator hose or a loose fan belt.

There's no way to look under the hood of AI programs—even the world's top scientists and mathematicians don't understand exactly how they work. As a species, we're moving swiftly into terra incognita, and we haven't yet invented a compass for finding our way home.

Back in the 1950s, science fiction writer Isaac Asimov proposed three laws of robotics that would keep people safe from their mechanical servants. Asimov's three laws pop up frequently in conversations about AI.

Unfortunately, the three laws don't exist in real life. Our legal relationships with AIs are similar to the user agreements we tend to accept automatically when we sign up for free software such as Gmail, Facebook, Twitter, and LinkedIn. We really don't know what we're agreeing to, what rights we're surrendering, and what risks we're accepting.

At least you can *see* robots. For the most part, AI is invisible. It's already programmed into many of the software products sold by major technology vendors, such as Apple, Google, Microsoft, IBM, Oracle, and Amazon. When young entrepreneurs seek funding from venture capitalists, there's invariably some kind of AI functionality built into whatever they're pitching. Very soon, AI will be baked into every product and service we use.

Most of the smart processes in smart cities will be managed by AIs. That's the reality we'll need to confront. AI is no longer science fiction—it's a rapidly growing part of our daily lives.

As a society, we need to set standards for AIs and hold them accountable for their decisions. We need ways of figuring out fast when AIs aren't working properly and we need techniques for replacing faulty AIs without jeopardizing the operational integrity of critical systems or putting people at risk.

Here are three key questions we need to ask about every AI:

1. Is it doing what it was created to do?

2. Can it explain its decisions?

3. Is it helping people—or hurting them?

Questions 1 and 3 should be easy to answer. Question 2 is the hard one, because most AIs cannot "explain" their decisions. AIs make decisions by sifting through mountains of data. AIs feed on big data—it's what makes them "smart." But the machine-learning processes required to train an AI are opaque to human beings—there is no way for us to peer into the "mind" of an AI and understand precisely how it reaches a conclusion.

Today, most AIs function like magical boxes—you put in data and they present you with results. Many people find the lack of transparency unsettling.

The general opacity of AI processes has led to a push for *explainable* or *interpretable* AI. It's too early to predict whether explainable AI will become the norm, but it feels like a step in the right direction.

Can We Prevent Crime Before It Happens?

Law enforcement has been using technology to solve crimes for more than a century. Using technology to *prevent* crimes, however, is a relatively new idea. The movie *Minority Report* famously depicts a futuristic society in which police officers arrest people *before* they commit crimes. It's a deeply disturbing movie with a not-too-subtle message about the danger of relying too heavily on technology.

Nevertheless, a small industry has emerged around the practice of predictive policing. New York, Chicago, Los Angeles, New Orleans, and other cities have experimented with predictive policing programs. The experiments have been inconclusive and controversial.

"Who's going to be the gatekeeper for these predictive technologies?" asks Andrew Guthrie Ferguson, professor of law at the University of the District of Columbia David A. Clarke School of Law and author of *The Rise of Big Data Policing*.

Ferguson is justifiably concerned that governments will buy complicated technology solutions from vendors without considering the potential downsides and long-term responsibilities, such as continually updating and refreshing the algorithms used in the solutions. In his book, he proposes that local, state, and federal governments hold annual "surveillance summits" to "audit, evaluate, and account for the big data police-surveillance technologies being used in the community."

Red Flags

As a culture, we tend to believe in the power of technology. So it's not surprising that we want to use technology for tackling social problems such as crime. But crime is a complex and multidimensional phenomenon. No two crimes are exactly alike. Sometimes they happen without warning; sometimes there are red flags.

In a free society, there's not much we can do to prevent spontaneous criminal behaviors. We can, however, do a much better job of spotting red flags, cataloging them, and responding more effectively when a series of red flags indicate that someone is likely to commit a violent crime in the near future.

Smart cities will unquestionably have the means to track and monitor people more effectively than ever before in history. An unanswered question is how far smart cities will go in their surveillance of individuals and groups. Our best guess is that each city will develop its own set of norms, based partly on culture and partly on economic needs. National governments might try to set standards, but the cities themselves will probably decide what levels of surveillance are appropriate and practical.

Will Smart Cities Respect Privacy?

Another unanswered question revolves around privacy. Is it reasonable to expect privacy in a city in which you're constantly monitored by cameras and sensors?

Jeffrey Blatt, an attorney specializing in cybersecurity and data privacy issues, describes himself as a "data privacy realist." He believes that it will become increasingly difficult to strike a balance between privacy and security in a world that depends so heavily on advanced digital technologies and massive data collection. "We are already seeing the balance tilt in favor of law enforcement and security," he says.

China's nascent Social Credit System, for example, uses data gleaned from surveillance cameras and financial, social media, and government databases to create "social credit scores" for Chinese citizens. The scores can be used to reward or punish certain types of behaviors, and to predict whether someone is likely to commit a crime. Blatt describes the system as "Orwell's *1984* on steroids."

Will smart cities follow China's example or will they find a middle path that respects privacy while maximizing operational efficiencies? Blatt doesn't hold out much hope for privacy.

"I fully understand and appreciate the efficiency and utility a smart city brings," Blatt says. "It will be a safer, cleaner, more efficient, and nicer place to live...but let's not fool ourselves—privacy and anonymity will be sacrificed."

Ferguson isn't quite as pessimistic. "You could build an architecture of privacy protections into your smart-city surveillance systems," Ferguson says. "But you have to build it at the front end and not wait until it's too late."

Too often, we think of privacy in terms of our relationships with consumer companies. In smart cities, however, the final arbiter of privacy will be the government, Ferguson says. Companies such as Amazon and Google could potentially embarrass you by releasing information about what you buy or what you search for on the Internet. "But the government can lock you up. That's the real difference—the power of the state to prosecute you."

Pushing Back

In all societies, citizens have duties and responsibilities. In smart cities, we'll be responsible for safeguarding our privacy and pushing back when we believe the government is encroaching on our rights. In some situations, of course, that will be easier said than done.

"You could move to another city," Ferguson says. "Maybe people will be able to choose between smart cities and not-so-smart cities. Maybe there will be areas where people will go to be free of surveillance."

As a society, we aren't thinking far enough ahead, he says. We're not debating or discussing issues that will surely arise as cities become increasingly smart. How much surveillance is too much? What's the right balance between security and liberty? Who decides?

In a true surveillance state, there will be very little crime. "But at what cost?" asks Ferguson.

Over the course of writing this book, we've had many conversations about the challenges of balancing a wide variety of essential needs, such as safety, security, efficiency, mobility, dignity, economic opportunity, sustainability, resiliency, privacy, and freedom. We don't believe in binary choices; it's never just a case of picking one or the other.

Smart cities will be laboratories for endless experiments. The experiments won't produce answers, but they will generate more questions. That's the nature of the scientific process. It's an ongoing quest for knowledge. Smart cities are part of that process. Because most of us will live in smart cities, we'll be participating directly in the experiments. We'll be affected personally, and the outcome of the experiments will matter to us.

For many people, the process will feel uncomfortable. Our best advice is to remain cautious and to always remember that we cannot delegate our human responsibilities to technology, no matter how advanced or infallible someone tells us it is. The responsibility for doing what's morally right will always rest on our shoulders, and that won't change, even in the smartest of cities.

In the next chapter, we'll look closely at the many ways in which smart cities can evolve and grow over time.

Endnote

1. http://www.newsweek.com/new-york-city-council-passes-law-curb-legionnaires-outbreak-362867

Chapter 11

Deceptive Complexity

WE BEGAN writing this book in the autumn of 2017. In some of our earliest interviews, we encountered skeptics who told us that the smart-city movement had hit a wall. The concept of smart cities, they said, was far too utopian for a world as unruly as ours.

In some respects, the skeptics were right. Local governments realized technology alone would not create smart communities and backed away from grandiose projects. The market for smart-city tech softened. Analysts who were bullish became bearish.

Despite the obstacles, the idea of smart cities remained alive. The road map, however, had changed. Instead of relying primarily on tech vendors, smart cities (and smart towns, states, counties, regions, and nations) began developing their own solutions.

Most of the projects we describe in this book are home-grown affairs. The initiatives in Tel Aviv, Barcelona, Dallas, and Estonia didn't rely on huge capital investments. In fact, they were accomplished with minimal funding.

The smart-city movement isn't dead—it's alive and well. The early version of the movement reflected the values and sensibilities of global technology vendors. Not surprisingly, the vendors saw smart cities as golden opportunities for selling products and services.

Today, smart cities are less dependent on the vendor community and much more willing to blaze their own trails. Smart cities draw inspiration from the maker movement, which takes pride in developing low-cost DIY solutions that can be easily upgraded or even scrapped when something new and better comes along.

Make no mistake: the smart-city movement hasn't become a free-for-all. There's still a road map, yet it's an updated version. The old version was mostly top-down; the newer version is a blend of bottom-up, top-down, and orthogonal inputs.

As we were wrapping up our research, we discovered an excellent post[1] co-authored by Josh Lieberman, a senior researcher at Harvard University's Center for Geographic Analysis. In the post, Lieberman and his co-author, Simon Chester, make the case for a Smart City Interoperability Reference Architecture (SCIRA). Here's a brief description of SCIRA from their post:

SCIRA will provide free deployment guides and reusable patterns that municipalities can use to plan, acquire, and implement standards-based, cost-effective, vendor-agnostic, and future-proof smart-city IT systems and networks using technologies such as Internet of Things (IoT), sensor webs, and geospatial information.

SCIRA defines interoperability requirements based on a system-of-systems approach for information technology in smart-city deployments, meaning that municipalities are able to build up smart cities little by little, project by project, safe in the knowledge that future expansions will work with, build upon, and gain value from the systems that they're implementing today.

We later spoke with Lieberman, who shared a fascinating insight: Smart cities are systems of systems operating at multiple scales. Different strategies and solutions are required to address challenges at different levels of scale. Operating at multiple scales simultaneously, however, requires degrees of integration and interoperability that would be difficult to achieve without an open, standards-based approach.

Why is an open standards-based approach necessary? There are several reasons. First, without an open standards-based approach, there's no guarantee that a solution provided by one vendor will work with a solution provided by another vendor. Second, an open standards-based approach makes it easier to modify, upgrade, and improve solutions that are already in place. Here's another brief excerpt from Lieberman and Chester's post:

> *For example, if a city implements citywide video feeds for monitoring transport flow and congestion, and then later wants to monitor pedestrian movement, there's a good chance that if proprietary formats were used in the initial monitoring system, the data will remain 'siloed' within that system. This would likely require the city to return to the original provider to purchase pedestrian monitoring software (if they sell it), or else install another set of cameras from another technology provider, with another separate back end to process the data, and then yet another system to join it all together.*
>
> *If, however, the video cameras are creating data in an open format, then any other analysis apps can just 'tap in' to that data feed—saving the city the cost of new hardware and increased data transport costs. This isn't just for video, but for any sensor or data collection device—from smart trash cans and lampposts, to air quality and water level monitors, and beyond.*

Neighborhood parking space systems, district-wide trash detection systems, and citywide 911 visualization systems are examples of separate systems operating at different scales that could utilize the same imaging assets if they were based on open formats and linked by open interfaces.

Open standards are crucial for interoperability, and interoperability is necessary for enabling agility, resiliency, and continuous improvement within complex smart-city ecosystems, Lieberman says (Figure 11.1).

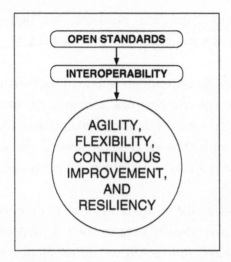

Figure 11.1 Open standards are crucial for interoperability
Source: Josh Lieberman.

In the remainder of this chapter, we look at the evolution of smart-city strategy and we outline the progressive stages of smart-city development. This next portion of the chapter was written by our good friends Alexander Gelsin, Bart Gorynski, and Thomas Müller, the co-founders of bee smart city,[2] a digital platform for facilitating collaboration and implementing smart-city solutions. If you are interested in smart-city solutions, we urge you to visit www.beesmart.city/index and search through its database.

Progressive Development

Smart cities enable their citizens to overcome challenges and seize opportunities to become more sustainable, more efficient, and more prosperous. In a very real and concrete manner, smart cities are platforms for helping citizens improve and elevate the quality of their lives.[3]

That sounds simple enough, although the path to becoming smarter is deceptively complex, requiring the skilled coordination of the activities of multiple stakeholders and the ability to juggle the simultaneous creation, testing, and scaling up of solutions that span an entire smart-city ecosystem.

In most cases, this means a lot of trial and error. A variety of solutions may already exist to solve a particular problem in different ways. New solutions are developed as each city optimizes life for its citizens and for its socially and culturally unique communities. As a result, many solutions have been tried and tested. It would be tempting to assume that a profusion of solutions means that choosing the right one will be easy. That, however, is not the case. Careful consideration is required to ensure that a solution is right for the target demographic.

General strategies for bringing cities forward have also changed over time, keeping pace with changing ideas of what a smart city should be and how it should develop. We think of this progression as the evolution of smart-city strategy.[4]

Evolving Strategies

How does a city become smarter? Urban strategist Boyd Cohen has identified three generations, or phases, of smart-city development.[5]

First-generation smart-city strategies are largely the result of partnerships between the city and major technology companies, and therefore seek to apply new technologies to solve urban problems as defined by the municipal government. Because the solutions provided under this kind of smart-city model can increase a city's day-to-day efficiency, this sort of top-down master plan typically appeals to municipalities at the beginning of their smart-city journey.

Technology, however, has since been reconsidered and redefined as an enabler rather than as a solution in itself. Born of this realization, second-generation strategies tend to focus on the application of technologies in enabling roles, where they can help to improve the quality of life for a city's residents; they do not, however, form a platform for a portfolio of smart-city solutions.

The role of technology in a second-generation strategy may not even go beyond facilitating connections among the different people working on a project. First- and second-generation strategies are driven primarily by the agendas of city governments—what's missing from both is the voice of citizens.

Third-generation strategies re-envision the smart-city model, placing the citizen at the center and recognizing the importance of the individual in the development and implementation of smart-city solutions tailored to the needs and priorities of the community itself. A citizen-centric focus can better engage the city's residents to participate in innovation and governance—in an "of the people, by the people, for the people" kind of way.

Adopting what could also be considered a user-centric model makes it easier to encourage the acceptance and uptake of new solutions across all demographics, as they are more likely to focus on the needs of the customer (the citizen) and will therefore be seen as having a clear purpose and benefit without any need for a hard sell. Such co-creation models can lead to more livable and prosperous urban communities.

Enter the Smartivist

A new role has appeared from within this third generation of smart-city strategies: that of the *smartivist*.[6] A smartivist can be someone who is highly motivated, highly skilled, or both. The smartivist can become a community leader in the innovation and uptake of smart-city solutions, either by stepping forward to support their creation and implementation, or by taking an active personal role in one of those processes.

Smartivists may act individually or by establishing co-creation initiatives, such as new associations or networks focused on finding solutions for specific problems. Working alone or in teams, they will be key enablers within their communities.

As previously mentioned, technology plays a supportive rather than a primary role in the development of smart cities. It's always important to remember that technology is an enabler, not a driver.

Technology must be subservient to human needs. A smart city relies on innovative ideas and solutions devised by a *quadruple helix* of stakeholders—government, businesses, members of academic and research institutions, and every one of the city's residents. Teamwork and collaboration among stakeholders in the community should drive smart-city development.

The single most important factor for the success of a third-generation smart city is, therefore, its ability to facilitate collaboration.[7] Once all stakeholders are ready and able to work together, the city can take its first steps toward growing smarter.

Defining the Smart-City Process

As a city begins its smart-city journey, there is a logical process it can follow. The first step is to determine the status quo—the city must decide where it is and where it wants to be.

A thorough assessment should be made of its current level of services and how they are being delivered, including their sustainability and whether or not they really meet the needs of the target demographic. Is perhaps a demographic being left out of a service that should be available to all citizens? Powerful enablers, such as the city's connectivity, both physical and digital, should also be considered, as should the quality of the city's health care and education services.

The many questions a city asks itself in this first step may produce some positive answers, and this will show the key strengths it has to build upon. This should already suggest some opportunities or advantages that can be leveraged in the second step: the detailed identification of problems and challenges that need solving in order to move the city closer to its goals.

The next part of the process is to prioritize these challenges and opportunities. In a third-generation smart city, deciding what problems to tackle and in what order is a collaborative process, though a recommended strategy is to look first for low-hanging fruit, allowing a city to direct its sometimes limited resources toward problems that could be quickly, easily, or cheaply resolved. This means faster improvements to the quality of life for its citizens.

The collaborative process should include the assessment of problems by citizens and their opinions about the urgency and importance of the challenges they are facing. Such a collaborative approach helps to identify dependent problems (whose solutions gradually resolve further problems), which is a big step toward becoming a smart city.

The last step is to implement solutions to the chosen problems. In some cases, solutions known to have been successful in other places can be adapted to suit similar situations; in other cases, innovation will be required in order to develop new, customized solutions.

In reality, these steps describe a continuous process of assessment, innovation, and action. To succeed, the focus of a smart-city strategy must be broad—not confined to just a single field of action.

Six Fields of Action

With the cooperative collaboration of all stakeholders, a city can be moved forward via innovations across six broad fields of action. We call these six fields *smart-city indicators*.

These fields, when developed together, form a holistic strategy.[8] The six fields cover the numerous aspects of urban life and echo Boyd Cohen's Smart Cities Wheel.[9]

A collective intelligence driving innovation across all six fields leads to the creation of a full ecosystem of smart-city solutions, with the needs of the citizens as the critical central focus.[10] Such a human-centric (user-centric) focus, coupled with an intelligent approach to solution implementation and the development and application of new technologies where appropriate, is a successful strategy for making cities smarter.

The following are brief sketches of each smart-city indicator. Over the next half decade, we expect dozens, or perhaps hundreds, of subcategories to emerge from each of the six indicators (Figure 11.2).

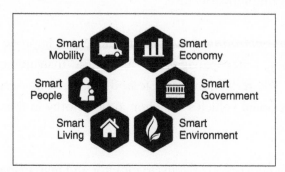

Figure 11.2 The six smart-city indicators
Source: bee smart city.

Smart Economy

Smart cities provide the right conditions for new and established businesses to grow and prosper. A city should strive to create a good climate for startups and other entrepreneurial activities, and to be attractive to investors as well as to highly skilled new talent, all of which should lead toward the overall goal of strengthening the city's economy and to the creation of new jobs.

It is not enough, however, simply to grow; a *smart economy* must be guided to transform and develop in sustainable directions. Actions that drive a smart economy generate stable, favorable conditions for all stakeholders.

Smart Environment

Urban planners need to maintain a balance between the built and natural environments in order to maximize the livability of the city for both residents and visitors. Standards should be established to minimize the environmental impact of new and existing infrastructure.

Smart-environment actions are those that improve energy efficiency, water management, and waste management processes. The reduction of waste and of emissions—especially from personal vehicles—is often a top priority in this field of action.

Using networked systems to monitor and help manage pollution as well as to transform a city's energy production and use support the cultural changes required to achieve a more sustainable urban way of life.

Smart Government

A *smart government* forges strong connections between itself and other stakeholders in a municipality. It builds trust through transparency and shared governance, adopting methodologies that allow and encourage citizen participation.

Smart-government solutions are those that improve the quality, accessibility, and scope of the municipal services on offer to businesses and individual residents. They should help to increase connectivity and ensure digital inclusion and equality, while keeping an eye on security and public safety.

By harnessing new technologies, offering city data via open-data platforms, and encouraging open innovation, a city government facilitates the creation of new smart-city solutions and increases its own efficiency and effectiveness.

Smart Living

Optimizing the living environment and the methods for its management for all age groups and demographics is the goal of *smart-living* actions, which will directly impact the quality of life for a city's residents. Electronic services, such as social platforms and solutions to increase digital inclusion are in focus, as are improved access to health care services and citizen safety.

Leveraging a wirelessly connected IoT and implementing smart buildings can create better housing and working conditions, as well as facilitate aged care or assisted living. Actions that enable and encourage civic and social engagement lead to smarter urban living.

Smart Mobility

Solutions that render urban transportation systems more efficient and that encourage their adoption by city residents in preference to the use of private vehicles are *smart-mobility* actions. They may improve the quality, broaden the accessibility, or reduce the cost of current transportation services, or they may provide entirely new mobility options.

Technologies to manage traffic intelligently and in real time can increase public safety while reducing journey times and vehicle emissions; the latter can also be achieved through the adoption of electric or autonomous vehicles, or by encouraging car- or bikesharing schemes. Smart-mobility actions must integrate multiple modes of transport for both people and goods across a city to create a smooth, customer-centric experience.

Smart People

The exchange of information among citizens and their lifelong education and employment opportunities are the key characteristics of *smart people*. Actions in this field transform the way people communicate both within and between communities, whether in the public or private sectors, leading to the more effective provision of information and services. This must be facilitated by educational services that improve social and digital inclusion and equality.

Implementing smarter education options and forging connections between educational institutions and potential employers can help to develop talent, support innovation, and take advantage of labor market opportunities. These actions generate an inclusive and creative learning climate, and enable the participation of all demographics to improve the prosperity of the city.

Toward the Fourth Generation of Smart Cities

It seems likely that smart-city strategies—from technology-driven (first generation) via technology enabled, city led (second generation) to citizen co-creation (third generation)—will continue to adapt and evolve. Based on the emergence of collective intelligence, which has been facilitated by advances in digital technologies and the internet a fourth generation can already be identified.

The fourth generation of smart cities is driven by the collective intelligence of all stakeholders, sourcing (best-practice) smart-city solutions, ideas, and knowledge globally via online platforms to accelerate the development of livable and prosperous cities and communities on the local level.

Sharing best practices and adapting or replicating proven solutions and new ideas is a logical next step from the third to the fourth generation of smart-city strategies. Online information and collaboration platforms, such as bee smart city, support efforts to make emerging smart-city ecosystems more transparent, responsive, agile, and adaptable.

Sooner or later, most of us will live in smart cities. It's up to us to determine whether those cities are smart because they're equipped with the latest technology solutions or smart because they provide us with the resources we need to live happy and fulfilling lives.

As they say in Barcelona, "We decide." If we take proactive roles and make smart-city planning a collaborative process, we can decide what kind of future we want for ourselves and for our descendants.

Endnotes

1. https://meetingoftheminds.org/a-technology-implementation-guide-for-smarter-cities-27139

2. https://beesmart.city/index

3. https://hub.beesmart.city/strategy/towards-a-new-paradigm-of-the-smart-city

4. https://hub.beesmart.city/strategy/a-review-of-becoming-a-smart-city

5. https://www.fastcompany.com/3047795/the-3-generations-of-smart-cities

6. https://hub.beesmart.city/smartivists/rise-of-the-smartivist-the-importance-of-smart-citizens-in-smart-cities

7. https://hub.beesmart.city/strategy/collective-intelligence-key-success-factor-for-the-smart-city

8. https://hub.beesmart.city/smart-city-indicators

9. https://www.smart-circle.org/smartcity/blog/boyd-cohen-the-smart-city-wheel

10. https://hub.beesmart.city/strategy/call-for-a-human-centric-smart-city-approach

Appendix A

Organizations and Councils

THIS IS a curated list of organizations, associations, councils, and partnerships providing information, services, and support for smart-city projects and initiatives. This is not intended to be a complete list; there are many excellent and helpful organizations in this field, and new ones emerge regularly.

American Public Transportation Association (APTA) is an association of public and private member organizations involved in light rail, commuter rail, buses, subways, paratransit, waterborne passenger services, and high-speed rail.

Association of Electronics, Information, and Communications Technologies, Telecommunications, and Digital Content Companies (AMETIC) champions the interests of Spanish businesses in technology and innovation. AMETIC represents a key sector for employment and competitiveness, with a major impact on Spain's GDP and excellent outsourcing possibilities for other production sectors.

Associació pel Desenvolupament Rural de la Catalunya Central is an association of primarily rural territories in central Catalonia aimed at incorporating efficient management procedures and promoting competitive and specialized business in leading or emerging sectors, such as agri-food, energy, forest resources, tourism, and industrial projects.

Berlin Partner for Business and Technology offers business and technology promotion for companies, investors, and science institutes in Berlin. The organization offers custom-tailored services and links to research; experts provide a wide range of offerings to help companies launch, innovate, expand, and secure their economic future in Berlin. A unique public-private partnership, it is a cooperative endeavor between the Berlin State Senate and over 200 companies dedicated to promoting Berlin.

British Standards Institution (BSI Group) is the national standards body of the UK. The organization offers certification programs, training courses, workshops, conferences, product launches, exhibitions, and a variety of other products and services in support of member businesses and quality standards.

Building Research Establishment (BRE) is a leading center of building science based in the UK. Established in 1921, BRE generates new knowledge through research and uses this knowledge to create new tools, products, and standards across the building industry. BRE is "an innovative group of researchers, scientists, engineers, and technicians who share a common goal—to make the built environment better for all," according to its website.[1]

Center for Urban Science and Progress (NYU CUSP) is a universitywide center whose research and education programs are focused on urban informatics. Using New York City as its lab and working from its base in the NYU Tandon School of Engineering, the center integrates and applies NYU strengths in the natural, data, and social sciences to understand and improve cities throughout the world.

Chicago Council on Global Affairs is a nonpartisan membership organization providing insight on critical global issues, convening global voices, conducting independent research, and engaging the public to explore ideas shaping the global future. "The Council is committed to bringing clarity and offering solutions to issues that transcend borders and transform how people, business, and governments engage the world," according to its website.

China Center for Urban Development (CCUD) is a public company established in 1998. The organization supplies policy documents and consultancy on urbanization, guidance to its pilot cities on urban reform and development, and plans for socioeconomic development and space and land use in China, East Asia, and the Pacific regions.

Circle Economy in the Netherlands is a community of businesses and institutions dedicated to accelerating the circular economy through promoting understanding of the circular economy and developing practical and scalable solutions to bring the concept of the circular, no-waste economy to fruition.

City Protocol is a community of practice and collaborative innovation framework that fosters "city-centric solutions which benefit citizens and their quality of life." It is oriented toward the Internet of Things as it applies to cities. According to the City Protocol website, its impact extends across "40 countries, 80 organizations, 350 experts, and 12 city projects."

City Tech - UI Labs is a partnership and collaboration creating solutions, services, and testbeds to remake and reinvent cities. Formed initially as Smart Chicago in 2010 to increase access to digital technologies, City Tech leverages technology to fuel business and employment opportunities, inclusion, engagement, and innovation.

EIT Digital brings together a partnership of over 130 European corporations, SMEs, startups, universities, and research institutes from its headquarters in Brussels. EIT Digital invests in strategic areas to accelerate market uptake of research-based digital technologies and to drive entrepreneurial talent and leadership in Europe.

Eurocities is a network of major European cities that provides a platform for its member cities to share knowledge and ideas, exchange experiences, analyze common problems, and develop innovative solutions through a wide range of forums, working groups, projects, activities, and events. Originally founded in 1986 by the mayors of Barcelona, Birmingham, Frankfurt, Lyon, Milan, and Rotterdam, today the organization brings together the local governments of more than 135 large cities in over 35 European countries from its headquarters in Brussels.

European Energy Efficiency Fund, headquartered in Luxembourg, is dedicated to mitigating climate change through energy efficiency measures and the use of renewable energy in Europe. It is an innovative public-private partnership and focuses on financing energy efficiency, small-scale renewable energy, and clean urban transport projects targeting municipal, local, and regional authorities and public and private entities that act on behalf of those authorities.

European Institute of Public Administration is a European center of expertise and exchange offering educational programs from locations in Maastricht, the Netherlands; Luxembourg; and Barcelona, Spain, concentrating in EU governance, policies, and public management. Areas of focus include courses, case studies, consulting services, and custom presentations.

European Patent Office is an intergovernmental organization headquartered in München, Germany. It supports innovation, competitiveness and economic growth across Europe through a commitment to high quality and efficient services delivered under the European Patent Convention.

European Telecommunications Standards Institute (ETSI) is an independent, not-for-profit, standardization organization in the telecommunications industry headquartered in Sophia-Antipolis, France. Established in 1988, it has produced over 30,000 standards and provides its (over 800) members with an open and inclusive environment to support and test "globally applicable standards across all sectors."

European Union Agency for Network and Information Security (ENISA) is an agency of the European Union and a center for cybersecurity expertise, network and information security, data protection issues, privacy, and emerging technologies. It is headquartered in Greece.

Fab Lab Barcelona is part of the Institute for Advanced Architecture of Catalonia, "where it supports different educational and research programs related with the multiple scales of the human habitat. It is also the headquarters of the global coordination of the Fab Academy program in collaboration with the Fab Foundation and the MIT's Center for Bits and Atoms." According to its website, the Fab Academy is "a distributed platform of education and research in which each Fab Lab operates as a classroom, and the planet [operates] as the campus of the largest university in construction in the world, where students learn about the principles, applications, and implications of digital manufacturing technology."

Future Cities Catapult is a UK, London-based think tank specializing in urban strategies, connected cities, and urban data science. Future Cities Catapult provides data analysis, modeling and visualization capabilities for innovative topics such as urban infrastructure, health, and urban mobility.

Institute for Advanced Architecture of Catalonia (IAAC) is an education and research center located in Barcelona, Spain, that promotes and develops architecture that is responsive to the worldwide challenges of livability and construction in the 21st century. The organization is known for its interaction with many disciplines, sponsorship of global competitions, and generation of new urban paradigms. Its mission includes "envisioning the future habitat of our society," and the organization follows every aspect of the digital revolution to expand the boundaries of architecture and design to create a new urban paradigm.

International Association of Public Transport (UITP) is a nonprofit advocacy organization that supports sustainable public transport and mobility in urban areas worldwide. Based in Brussels, it has 1,500 member companies and provides networking of over 18,000 contacts to its members from 96 countries. The organization includes public-transport authorities, policy decision-makers, scientific and research institutes, and public transportation, service, and supply firms.

International Electrotechnical Commission (IEC) is an international standards organization that develops and maintains standards for a hybrid set of electric, electromagnetic, and related technologies. Included in the scope of the organization's activities is a technology section with sites dedicated to smart cities, smart grids, and energy.

International Organization for Standardization (ISO) is "an independent, nongovernmental international organization with a membership of 160 national standards bodies." The ISO "brings together experts to share knowledge and develop voluntary, consensus-based, market-relevant international standards that support innovation and provide solutions to global challenges," according to its website. These standards are "world-class specifications for products, services, and systems" for ensuring "quality, safety, and efficiency. They are instrumental in facilitating international trade."

Internet Engineering Task Force (IETF) sponsors events and conferences for an international community of network designers, operators, and researchers about the evolution of the Internet and its architectural oversight. The IETF created and published the new Internet standard and set of specifications for Internet Protocol Version 6, IPv6, that expands the IP addresses that were available in IPv4 from 32 bits to the 128 bits now available in IPv6. This upgrade provides for Internet growth and the new IP addresses needed for the connectivity of an ever-expanding number of computing devices.

Israel Smart Cities Institute (ISCI) offers consulting and management services for smart cities. Delivered through a team of experts from the academic, technological, industrial, business, legal, and municipal areas, expertise is provided in a wide range of smart-city services, including energy, transportation, environmental protection, water and agriculture, planning for sustainable results, policies, e-governance implementation, smart education, technology, telecommunications infrastructure, mobility, and other smart-city services.

Leading Cities is a network of cities focused on smart-city solutions, city diplomacy, and collaboration advancing sustainability and resilient city strategies and technologies. Leading Cities has built bridges to share best practices, urban solutions, and lessons learned among city leaders while breaking down barriers within cities by engaging each of the five sectors of the Quintuple-helix (Q-helix): public, private, nonprofit, academia, and citizenry.

Local Governments for Sustainability (ICLEI) leads a global network of more than 1,500 cities, towns, and regions committed to building a sustainable future.

Meeting of the Minds is a global leadership network and knowledge-sharing platform focused on urban sustainability, connected technology, and (in particular) innovation for smart cities. Based in San Francisco, the organization extends across geographies and showcases ideas and practical solutions that can be replicated and scaled.

Moscow Agency of Innovations was founded by the Department of Science, Industrial Policy, and Entrepreneurship as a one-stop shop for participants in Moscow's innovation ecosystem. It includes public-private partnerships. Stated goals include providing services to innovation companies, public organizations, and youth interested in science, innovation, and advanced technologies.

National Institute of Standards and Technology (NIST) is an agency of the US Commerce Department. NIST's mission, according to its website, is promoting "US innovation and industrial competitiveness by advancing measurement science, standards, and technology in ways that enhance economic security and improve our quality of life. NIST's efforts include stimulating innovation, fostering industrial competitiveness and improving quality of life. Its core competencies include measurement science, rigorous traceability, and the development and use of standards.

National League of Cities (NLC) is an advocacy group for local governments in the United States. The NLC is "dedicated to helping city leaders build better communities," according to its website. The organization "serves as a resource to and an advocate for the more than 19,000 cities, villages, and towns it represents."

Nesta is a global, not-for-profit innovation foundation based in the UK. The organization practices *futurescoping*: exploring emerging technologies and groundbreaking ideas to tackle the challenges of the future. Nesta operates across the globe and across multiple sectors, including health, education, government, the broad economy, culture, and innovation policy.

Object Management Group (OMG) is an international, open membership, not-for-profit technology standards consortium with representation from government, industry, and academia. OMG task forces develop enterprise integration standards for a wide range of technologies and industries, such as health care, space, military, finance, government, retail, and workplace benefits. Examples of OMG standards include OMG Unified Modeling Language (UML), OMG Systems Modeling Language (SysML), OMG Data-Distribution Service (DDS), OMG Common Object Requirements Broker Architecture (CORBA), and OMG Business Process Modeling Notation (BPMN).

Open & Agile Smart Cities (OASC) is an organization of members from 117 cities of 24 countries and regions in Europe, Latin America, and Asia-Pacific. It features various information, news, events, a blog, and articles of interest to the converging IoT and Smart Cities communities. Head-quartered in Brussels, it is a city-driven initiative to create a global smart-city market (#smartcity) based on minimal interoperability mechanisms.

Open Geospatial Consortium (OGC) is an international not-for-profit consortium of over 520 companies, government organizations, and universities committed to setting and maintaining quality open standards for the global geospatial community that are vendor neutral. OGC standards work as interoperable solutions for data display and mapping. Their utility derives from geo-enabling the web, wireless, and other location-based services used across multiple domains.

Skolkovo Foundation is the managing entity for the Skolkovo Innovation Center. It is charged with providing catalysts to diversify the Russian economy. Its overarching goal is to create a sustainable ecosystem of entrepreneurship and innovation, engender a startup culture for venture capitalism, and stimulate the development of breakthrough projects and technologies.

Smart Africa Alliance is a Rwanda-based group and framework for developing Africa through information and telecommunications. Its work implements goals set forth in the African Manifesto, a 2014 agreement among African nation signatories, the World Bank, the African Development Bank, and others to place ICT at the center of Africa's socioeconomic agenda, improve access to ICT, especially broadband technology, and improve accountability, efficiency, and openness for sustainable development.

Smart Cities Council is "a network of leading companies advised by top universities, laboratories, and standards bodies." It provides readiness guides, financing templates, policy frameworks, case studies, visibility campaigns, and regional networking events that help cities "tap into the transformative power of smart technologies."

Sounds of New York City (SONYC) is an urban informatics project of New York University's Center for Urban Science and Progress (NYU CUSP) that monitors noise pollution in New York City. The project is a joint effort of a team of scientists from NYU and collaborators at Ohio State University working together in a first-of-its-kind, comprehensive research initiative to understand and address noise pollution in New York and beyond.

Sustainable Cities Program, launched in 2016, is supported by the City of Aalborg, Denmark, the Basque Country, and ICLEI Europe. Headquartered in Freiburg, Germany, the organization consists of 488 cities/regions and 127 organizations that constitute an information hub for local governments around the *Basque Declaration* and the *Transformative Actions Database* and sustainability.

United States Conference of Mayors (USCM) is a Washington, D.C.–based organization of cities with populations of 30,000 or more. The USCM covers a broad range of topics including immigration, crime, health, the environment, the urban workforce, waste management, water, transportation, communications, city design, and sustainability. The organization holds events, organizes task forces, and serves as an information-sharing resource for cities.

World Smart City is a partnership between the IEC (International Electrotechnical Commission), the ISO (International Organization for Standardization), and the ITU (International Telecommunication Union). The objective of World Smart City is helping smart cities become a reality through a common approach founded on standards. The main goal of the partnership is understanding and meeting the needs of stakeholders and developing consensus-based standards of good practice that address urban challenges and create common markets. The organization provides its members and customers in smart-city communities with real-world answers that can be understood and put into practice.

Endnote

1. https://bregroup.com/about-us

Appendix B

Conferences and Events

THE FOLLOWING is a list of select conferences and events focused on smart cities and urban development. It is not a comprehensive list, but rather a starting point for your own research.

Chicago Forum on Global Cities is an international conference hosted by the Chicago Council on Global Affairs and the *Financial Times*. The forum "raises provocative questions about the influence of global cities and how they can solve pressing global challenges" and includes in-depth panel discussions moderated by *Financial Times* journalists, "flash talks," intensive workshops, and informal networking for participating thought leaders and decision makers.

Internet of Things Solutions World Congress (IoTSWC) is held annually in Barcelona, Spain, in partnership with the Industrial Internet Consortium (IIC) and Fira Barcelona. The IoTSWC is a comprehensive program of presentations, keynote speeches, conferences, exhibits, testbeds, and an innovation awards ceremony.

Nordic Smart Cities Conference & Expo in Malmö, Sweden, brings together more than 100 speakers from cities, municipalities, academia, and industry. It features case studies and forecasts on the future of smart-city development.

Smart Cities Connect Conference & Expo is a US-based conference series at which companies display innovative products and municipal leaders share smart-city ideas and best practices, policies, and technologies.

Smart City Expo World Congress is an annual conference held in Barcelona, Spain, at Fira Barcelona, a premier conference venue. Since the first congress in 2011, the event has brought together urban planners, architects, government leaders, technology innovators, and companies of all sizes from start-ups to established firms, all dedicated to promoting awareness, understanding, and critical reflection among inhabitants of different cities worldwide. The event serves as a platform for creating a better future for global cities and their citizens.

Smart Cities Expo World Forum in Melbourne, Australia, "combines the power of co-located conference with state-of-the-art expo floor in order to educate people toward smart cities and urban planning technologies, strive for innovation, promote business, and connect thousands of attendees from around the globe." The conference program covers vertical applications in areas such as smart grid, smart transportation, smart health, Industry 4.0, artificial intelligence, virtual reality, cloud computing, smart building-management systems, enterprise IoT, fog computing, big-data analytics, and smart governance.

Smart Cities Innovation Summit Asia in Goyang, South Korea, gathers mayors, council members, sustainability officers, water and energy managers, urban designers, public works managers, and IT architects. The conference showcases products and services for building smart infrastructure, mobility, building, and energy.

Smart Cities NY is an annual conference bringing together global industry leaders, technology pioneers, city and government officials, and thought leaders to share knowledge and best practices at workshops, conferences, and panel discussions on public-private partnerships, technology for social good, sustainability, resilience, and inclusion in smart cities.

Smart Cities Summit in Atlanta is colocated with Industrial IoT World and IoT Blockchain Summit. The summit focuses on resiliency and responsiveness. Tracks include municipalities, connectivity, digital transformation, and citizens in cities. Topics within the tracks include public-private partnerships; funding, regulation and standardization; utilizing big data; connected and sustainable infrastructure; cybersecurity; AR/VR and blockchain; AI, applications and automation; drones and the future; improving the urban environment; seamless transportation; and public safety.

Smart Country Convention in Berlin focuses on digital solutions for administrations and public services in municipalities, regions and national governments. The event combines networking and training opportunities, and includes a lecture program and specialist congress. "Key players from administrations, government agencies, the digital economy, associations, and science come together on three days with one common goal: digitization of the entire public sector," according to the event's website.

World Cities Summit in Singapore "explores how cities can be more livable and resilient through better governance and planning, technology, and social innovations, as well as collaborations with various stakeholders with other cities. Through shared vision and active engagement, the public, private, and people sectors can co-create innovative and integrated urban solutions for a more sustainable future."

GLOSSARY

THE FOLLOWING is a list of terms that are typically used in articles and conversations about smart cities. This is by no means a comprehensive or exhaustive list; please use the list as a starting point for your own research and study.

5G (fifth-generation) wireless broadband will offer data transfer speeds significantly faster than 4G and 3G, shorter latency when sending and receiving data, and greater connectivity among devices, infrastructure, and people. It is seen by many as a foundational technology component of smart-city development and is expected by be deployed widely over the next five years.

Actuators are devices that move or control mechanisms, such as electric motors. Increasingly driven by software, actuators can be hydraulic, pneumatic, electric, thermal, or mechanical.[1]

Adaptive signal control combines artificial intelligence, systems of multiple sensors, and traffic signals to manage traffic flow and reduce congestion in real time. Surtrac (Scalable Urban TRAffic Control) and SCOOT (Split Cycle and Offset Optimisation Technique) are examples of advanced traffic management systems using adaptive signal control methods.

Agritecture is a term denoting the convergence of architecture and agriculture. "Agritecture" is the art, science, and practice of incorporating agriculture into the built environment. This integration can be inside of the building (indoor vertical farming) to maximize the density of growing, or outside of it (living walls and rooftop farms) to take advantage of the microclimates that exist through the design of city architecture," according to the Vertical Farming Academy.[2]

Algorithms are step-by-step sets of instructions used for solving problems. Algorithms will become integral to smart cities, automating and optimizing a broad variety of essential functions, such as trash collection, road maintenance, transit routing, and traffic signals.

Bicing is a popular bicycle-sharing program in Barcelona, Spain. Similar programs have been implemented in Paris and Stockholm. Bicing and other bikesharing systems are intended to help cities to reduce traffic congestion, improve air quality, provide opportunities for exercise, and offer viable alternatives to motor vehicle transportation.

Blockchain is the foundational technology of cryptocurrencies, such as Bitcoin. As a distributed ledger, however, blockchain has the potential for shaping the future of smart cities. Blockchain enables the creation of permanent records that are highly resistant to tampering, which means it can be used to support critical record-keeping functions in a variety of key areas, such as tax collection, land management, court administration, and voting registration.

Building Research Establishment Environmental Assessment Method (BREEAM) is the world's longest standing method for rating and certifying the sustainability of buildings. BREEAM is an essential part of the smart-city movement, since it provides scientific standards for assessing levels and degrees of sustainability in buildings and structures. BREEAM is used in 76 countries, including the UK, United States, the Netherlands, Spain, Norway, Sweden, Switzerland, and Austria.[3]

Circular economy is an increasingly popular concept that replaces traditional cycles of "take, make and dispose" with a new paradigm focused on restoration and regeneration. Instead of assuming a linear flow from *cradle to grave*, circular economies are based on *cradle-to-cradle* models of resource management that allow for *upcycling* and "a positive recoupling of the relationship between economy and ecology."[4]

Clean energy includes wind, solar, biomass, energy from the ocean, geothermal, and gravitational energy. Nuclear energy is considered clean by some experts, but the radioactive waste it leaves behind disqualifies it as truly clean.

Complete streets are intentionally designed and operated to enable safe access for all users, including pedestrians, bicyclists, motorists, and transit riders of all ages and abilities.[5] They are considered essential for reducing the number of traffic accidents and the severity of traffic-related injuries.

Congestion pricing is a strategy used by cities mostly in city centers and business districts to reduce motor vehicle traffic. It typically relies on charging drivers extra fees for operating motor vehicles in certain areas of a city during specific hours of the workweek.

DevOps, short for development and operations, was created to lower barriers between phases of software creation and implementation, ideally making it easier and more efficient to migrate, test, and deploy code.

Geographic information systems (GISs) assemble, store, manipulate, analyze, manage, and display multiple types of geographic data and information, making it easier to plan development, maintain infrastructure, and coordinate emergency operations.[6] GIS is rapidly emerging as a critical technology for planning, developing, and managing smart cities.

Human-centered design reverses the traditional design process by initially considering the user experience and then designing the product or service to meet the needs and expectations of users. This approach to design will become absolutely essential for smart cities as they develop and deploy new technologies for residents and visitors.

Interoperability refers to the ability of different components, computers, and systems to share resources and exchange information, so they can work together effectively and with minimal constraints across a variety of networks. The concept of interoperability is important to smart cities because they will invariably deploy technology systems and solutions from multiple vendors and sources, and those technology resources will need to interact and interoperate seamlessly.

Jane Jacobs was a journalist and urban activist who advocated for grassroots, community-based approaches to city planning and development. She was a vocal and effective opponent of large-scale, top-down, bureaucratic solutions that disregarded the value and vitality of smaller neighborhoods and communities within the urban landscape. Her legendary battles have informed and inspired a new generation of smart-city planners. Published in 1961, *The Death and Life of Great American Cities* is required reading for smart-city enthusiasts.

Last mile traditionally refers to the final connection between a telecommunication service provider and a customer, but it is now used increasingly in urban transit scenarios to describe any distance between an endpoint of a transportation service and a traveler's intended destination. In other words, if you drive your car to work, the *last mile* is the distance between where you park and where your office is. The term in often used in conjunction with "first mile," which refers to the distance between a traveler's home or point of origin and the traveler's preferred mode of public transportation (e.g., bus, train, subway, etc.).

Leadership in Energy and Environmental Design (LEED) is the "most widely used green building rating system in the world." Used in more than 165 countries and territories, LEED provides a practical framework for creating "healthy, highly efficient, and cost-saving green buildings" and is a "globally recognized symbol of sustainability achievement," according to the LEED website.[7]

LIDAR (Light Detection and Ranging) is a technology for using light to measure distances. It has become a critical enabling technology for self-driving cars and other autonomous vehicles. LIDAR can detect other vehicles, bicyclists, and pedestrians, and provide alerts to the driver or initiate maneuvers to avoid collisions.

Open source refers primarily to computer code that is publicly accessible and can be freely shared, as opposed to proprietary software, which is owned by a private entity and strictly controlled. Because open-source software can be modified and adapted for a variety of uses, it plays an important role in technology innovation and improvement processes. Linux is an example of a widely used open-source operating system.

Public-private partnerships, also known as PPPs or P3s, combine public- and private-sector resources. P3s can be used for financing, building, and operating public-use projects, such as parks, playgrounds, pedestrian malls, bike paths, parking garages, bike paths, and microtransit services. They offer an attractive alternative to traditional forms of financing and operating public-use projects.

Sensors measure and detect conditions in the physical world, such as motion, heat, moisture, light, and acceleration, and convert those inputs into electronic signals that can be sent to a processor or database.

Sharing economy is a term used to describe a wide range of new business models for creating value from underutilized assets, such as automobiles, bicycles, homes, office space, and even clothing. Some of the best-known examples of the sharing economy are Uber, Lyft, Airbnb, and WeWork. The concepts and models pioneered by firms in the sharing economy are also used in the so-called *gig economy*, which is essentially a mechanism for matching people with talent and free time with people who need their services on a temporary basis.

Smart buildings use a variety of technologies and data analysis techniques to automate and control systems for ventilation, heating, air conditioning, lighting, security, and energy consumption. In addition to digital technologies, smart buildings also make use of passive strategies for regulating temperature and conserving energy, such as room location, roof overhang, convective heat transfer, specially treated windows, and choice of materials. Leading examples of smart buildings are The Edge in Amsterdam, the Bullitt Center in Seattle, Siemens City in Vienna, and Capital Tower in Singapore.

Sustainable Development Goals (SDGs) are part of the United Nation's 2030 Agenda for Sustainable Development,[8] which builds on the principle of "leaving no one behind" and emphasizes a holistic approach to achieving sustainable development for all. The 17 goals are:

1. No Poverty

2. Zero Hunger

3. Good Health and Well-being

4. Quality Education

5. Gender Equality

6. Clean Water and Sanitation

7. Affordable and Clean Energy

8. Decent Work and Economic Growth

9. Industry, Innovation, and Infrastructure

10. Reduced Inequality

11. Sustainable Cities and Communities

12. Responsible Consumption and Production

13. Climate Action

14. Life below Water

15. Life on Land

16. Peace and Justice Strong Institutions

17. Partnerships to Achieve the Goals

Warhol economy is a term coined by urban planning professor Elizabeth Currid in her 2007 book, *The Warhol Economy: How Fashion, Art, and Music Drive New York City.* It describes how a combination of creative cultures fuel Manhattan's economy.

Endnotes

1. https://www.techopedia.com/definition/17043/actuator

2. https://academy.vertical-farming.net/intro-to-agritecture

3. https://www.breeam.com/location

4. https://www.ellenmacarthurfoundation.org/circular-economy/interactive-diagram/efficiency-vs-effectiveness

5. https://smartgrowthamerica.org/program/national-complete-streets-coalition/publications/what-are-complete-streets

6. https://www.gislounge.com/what-is-gis

7. https://new.usgbc.org/leed

8. https://www.un.org/development/desa/disabilities/envision2030.html

RECOMMENDED READING

Nonfiction

Alexander, Christopher. *A City Is Not a Tree*. Portland, OR: Sustasis Press, 2015.

Barlow, Mike. *Learning to Love Data Science: Explorations of Emerging Technologies and Platforms for Predictive Analytics, Machine Learning, Digital Manufacturing, and Supply Chain Optimization*. Sebastopol, CA: O'Reilly Media, 2015.

Brynjolfsson, Erik, and Andrew McAfee. *The Second Machine Age: Work, Progress, and Prosperity in a Time of Brilliant Technologies*. New York: W. W. Norton, 2014.

Caro, Robert A. *The Power Broker: Robert Moses and the Fall of New York*. New York: Vintage Books, 1975.

Cerdà, Ildefons. *General Theory of Urbanization*. New York: Actar, 2018 (originally published in 1867).

Currid, Elizabeth. *The Warhol Economy: How Fashion, Art, and Music Drive New York City*. Princeton, NJ: Princeton University Press, 2007.

Eubanks, Virginia. *Automating Inequality: How High-Tech Tools Profile, Police, and Punish the Poor*. New York: St. Martin's Press, 2017.

Ferguson, Andrew Guthrie. *The Rise of Big Data Policing: Surveillance, Race, and the Future of Law Enforcement*. New York: New York University Press, 2017.

Florida, Richard. *The Rise of the Creative Class—Revisited*. New York: Basic Books, 2012.

Garvin, Alexander. *The American City: What Works, What Doesn't*, 3rd ed. New York: McGraw-Hill Education, 2014.

Glaeser, Edward. *Triumph of the City: How Our Greatest Invention Makes Us Richard, Smarter, Greener, Healthier, and Happier*. New York: Penguin Group, 2011.

Goldstein, Brett, and Lauren Dyson (eds.). *Beyond Transparency: Open Data and the Future of Civic Innovation*. San Francisco: Code for America Press, 2013.

Gratz, Roberta Brandes. *The Battle for Gotham: New York in the Shadow of Robert Moses and Jane Jacobs*. New York: Nation Books, 2010.

Hughes, Robert. *Barcelona*. New York: Vintage Books, 1992.

Jacobs, Jane. *The Death and Life of Great American Cities*. New York: Vintage Books, 1992 (originally published in 1961).

Katz, Bruce, and Jeremy Nowak. *The New Localism: How Cities Can Thrive in the Age of Populism*. Washington, DC: Brookings Institution, 2017.

Koppel, Ted. *Lights Out*. New York: Crown, 2015.

Kropotkin, Peter. *Mutual Aid: A Factor in Evolution*. North Charleston, SC: CreateSpace Independent Publishing Platform, 2014.

Lacy, Peter, and Jakob Rutqvist. *Waste to Wealth: The Circular Economy Advantage*. New York: Palgrave Macmillan, 2015.

Manchester, William. *A World Lit Only by Fire: The Medieval Mind and the Renaissance, Portrait of an Age*. New York: Back Bay Books, 1992.

O'Neil, Cathy. *Weapons of Math Destruction: How Big Data Increases Inequality and Threatens Democracy*. New York: Broadway Books, 2017.

Pasher, Edna, and Tuvya Ronen. *The Complete Guide to Knowledge Management: A Strategic Plan to Leverage Your Company's Intellectual Capital*. Hoboken, NJ: Wiley, 2011.

Pentland, Alex. *Social Physics: How Social Networks Can Make Us Smarter*. New York: Penguin Books, 2014, 2015.

Sennett, Richard. *Building and Dwelling: Ethics for the City*. New York: Farrar, Straus and Giroux, 2018.

Sennett, Richard, Ricky Burdett, and Saskia Sassen, in dialogue with Joan Clos. *The Quito Papers and the New Urban Agenda*. New York: Routledge, 2018.

Senor, Dan, and Saul Singer. *Start-Up Nation: The Story of Israel's Economic Miracle*. New York: Twelve, 2009, 2011.

Sharkey, Patrick. *Uneasy Peace: The Great Crime Decline, the Renewal of City Life, and the Next War on Violence*. New York: W.W. Norton, 2018.

Taleb, Nassim Nicholas. *Fooled by Randomness: The Hidden Role of Chance in Life and in the Markets*. New York: Random House Trade Paperbacks, 2004.

Townsend, Anthony M. *Smart Cities: Big Data, Civic Hackers, and the Quest for a New Utopia*. New York: W. W. Norton, 2014.

Fiction

Asimov, Isaac. *Caves of Steel*. New York: Bantam Spectra, 1991 (originally published in 1953).

Bellamy, Edward. *Looking Backward*. Mineola, New York: Dover Publications, 1996 (originally published in 1888).

Dick, Philip K. *Do Androids Dream of Electric Sheep?* New York: Random House, 1968.

Gibson, William. *Neuromancer*. New York: Ace Books, 2000.

Huxley, Aldous. *Brave New World*. New York: Harper Perennial, 2006 (originally published in 1932).

Lob, Jacques, and Jean-Marc Rochette. *Snowpiercer.* Vol. 1, *The Escape*. Dallas, TX: Titan Comics, 2014.

Miéville, China. *The City & The City*. New York: Random House, 2010.

Mitchell, Stephen. *Gilgamesh/A New English Version*. New York: Free Press, 2004.

Orwell, George. *1984*. New York: New American Library, 1977 (originally published in 1949).

Reeve, Philip. *Mortal Engines*. London: Scholastic, 2001.

Stephenson, Neal. *Seveneves*. New York: HarperCollins, 2015.

Wells, H. G. *The Shape of Things to Come*. London: Penguin Classics, 2005 (originally published in 1933).

MEET OUR EXPERT SOURCES

Hannes Astok

Hannes Astok is a senior expert and deputy director for strategy and development at the Estonian e-Governance Academy (www.ega.ee). He provides training and consultancy for governments in Central Asia, the Caucasus, Southeast Europe, the Middle East, Africa, and other transition regions. Recently, he has been working closely with the governments of Ukraine, Namibia, Moldova, Palestine, Georgia, and Mauritius, among others.

Astok is an enthusiastic speaker for the "information society," especially promoting the role of local governments and describing the challenges of mobile governance and new technologies in government.

He was a member of the Estonian Parliament (Riigikogu) from 2007 to 2011 and deputy mayor of Estonia's second-largest city, Tartu, from 1997 to 2005. As a member of parliament, he dealt mainly with the development of the information society, issues related to the regulation of intellectual property, and electronic communication issues.

From 2012 to 2013, Astok was an adviser to the president of Estonia on the development of the nation's information society.

Astok began his political career in Tartu, serving as the city of Tartu's deputy mayor for almost a decade. Today, Tartu is one of the world's leading cities in e-governance, providing for citizens and businesses wide variety of internet and mobile phone-based services.

Astok holds a degree from Tartu University in journalism and public relations. He speaks Estonian, English, Russian, and Finnish.

Xabier E. Barandiaran

Xabier E. Barandiaran is a philosopher of mind and a philosopher of biological, cognitive, and social sciences, with a special focus on complex system analysis and conceptual simulation modeling for theory construction. He obtained an MSc with distinction in evolutionary and adaptive systems from the University of Sussex (Brighton, UK) and a PhD with distinction cum laude in philosophy of science and cognitive systems, as well as an outstanding doctorate award (*premio extraordinario*) for best humanities PhD thesis 2008, from the University of the Basque Country (UPV/EHU) in Spain.

He was a visiting researcher at the Konrad Lorenz Institute (Austria) and at the Autonomous Systems Lab, Polytechnic University (Madrid). He received a postdoctoral research fellowship from the Spanish Ministry of Science and undertook research at both the Centre for Computational Neuroscience and Robotics and COGS (University of Sussex, UK) and the Centre de Recherche en Epistemologie Appliquée, CNRS (Ecole Polytechnique, Paris, France). Subsequently, he returned to the UPV/EHU as a postdoctoral researcher for the FP7 research project Extending SensoriMotor Contingencies to Cognition.

Barandiaran has been a lecturer in the Department of Philosophy, UPV/EHU, for the past four years. In April 2016, he took an unpaid leave to become head of the Barcelona City Council's Research, Development and Innovation Directorate for Citizen Rights, Participation and Transparency, leading a number of research projects, including the design and service deployment of the Decidim, Barcelona's digital platform for participatory democracy, and managing 2 million euros over the 2016–2018 period.

He has more than 45 indexed publications in peer-reviewed journals, book chapters, and conference proceedings, totaling 989 citations and an h-index of 17, according to Google Scholar (46 publications, 22 with citation data, 310 citations, an h-index of 9, and 14.09 average citations per article, according to ResearcherID/ISI Web of Knowledge). Of these, 17 publications are in Q1 journals in the areas of philosophy, psychology, social sciences, and cognitive and neural sciences.

In addition, Barandiaran has been directly awarded seven distinct grants and has actively participated in 14 different research projects.

He has also organized several national workshops, summer schools, and conferences, as well as two international summer schools, four international workshops, and one international conference.

Jeffrey Blatt

Jeffrey Blatt is a California technology lawyer and board member with over 35 years of experience assisting technology, media, and telecom companies in the United States and Asia. He is a Silicon Valley pioneer, who has worked directly with the founders of key tech companies, including Apple, Sun Microsystems, Intel, and Broadcom.

In addition to his background in law and engineering, he is also a part-time California law enforcement officer with extensive training in cyber investigations and is certified in California to participate in electronic interception. A significant component of his international practice involves the issues of cybersecurity, data privacy, lawful government access to data, and risk mitigation strategies.

He is a frequent speaker at international conferences on the subject of data privacy and government surveillance and has authored a variety of items on the subject, including "Government Surveillance, Security, and Privacy: Does Security Always Win?" (Data Privacy Asia; June 17, 2017), "In Tech We Trust: Securing Digital Privacy in a Global Surveillance State" (RSA Asia Pacific Japan 2017), and "1984 Redux: China's Social Credit System a Harbinger of the Future" (RSA Asia Pacific Japan 2018).

Blatt earned a JD degree from the Lewis and Clark Law School in Portland, Oregon, graduating cum laude. He also obtained a BS in engineering from the University of California,

Los Angeles, and an MS, with highest distinction, in criminal justice/security studies from Tiffin University, Ohio.

He is a member of the California Bar and a licensed US patent attorney. As of this writing, he is Of Counsel at Tilleke & Gibbins in Bangkok, Thailand. He has previously held senior management and board positions at major telecom and broadcasting enterprises in Asia. Blatt is a former partner at the nationally recognized law firm of Irell & Manella in Los Angeles.

Francesca Bria

Francesca Bria is a senior researcher and adviser on information and technology policy. She has a PhD in innovation economics from Imperial College, London, and an MSc in digital economy from the University of London, Birbeck.

As senior program lead at Nesta, the UK innovation foundation, she led the EU D-CENT project, the largest project on direct democracy and digital currencies in Europe. Previously, she led the DSI (Digital Social Innovation) project in Europe, advising the EU on digital social innovation policies. She currently teaches in several universities in the UK and in Italy, and she has advised governments, public and private organizations, and movements on technology and information policy, and its socioeconomic impact.

Bria is an adviser to the European Commission on Future Internet and Innovation Policy. She is currently the chief technology and digital information officer for the City of Barcelona, Spain.

Boyd Cohen

Boyd Cohen, PhD, is an urban strategist focused on the areas of urban innovation, entrepreneurship, smart cities, and the Internet of Mobility. He has published three books: *Climate Capitalism* (2011); *The Emergence of the Urban Entrepreneur* (2016); and *Post-Capitalist Entrepreneurship* (2017).

Cohen is Dean of Research at EADA Business School and jointly appointed at the University of Victoria (UVic).

In 2017, he co-founded IoMob.net, a blockchain startup seeking to decentralize the mobility sector by providing an open protocol for the Internet of Mobility (IoM).

Di-Ann Eisnor

Di-Ann Eisnor is currently incubating new urban systems at Google's Area 120. Eisnor started the US office of Waze in 2009 and was Director of Growth for the crowd-sourced navigation and real-time traffic application, including platform, business development, and marketing. Waze was acquired by Google in 2013.

While at Waze, Eisnor founded the Waze Connected Citizens Program, which worked with 650 cities and departments of transportation to use data to reduce congestion and improve emergency response times.

Prior to joining Waze, Eisnor was co-founder and CEO of Platial, The People's Atlas, a collaborative, user-generated, cartographic website that enabled people to map the things that are important to them. She serves on the board of Saia Inc. (NASDAQ: SAIA), Gray Area Foundation for the Arts, and MeetUp Inc. She is an active angel investor and speaks widely on mobility, cities, and crowdsourcing.

Along with Lupe Fiasco, she is co-founder of Neighborhood Start Fund, a neighborhood-based microfund in underserved urban neighborhoods. Eisnor holds a BS in Studio Art and Business Administration from New York University. She is a 2014 Henry Crown Fellow of the Aspen Institute and a member of the Aspen Global Leadership Network.

Andrew Guthrie Ferguson

Andrew Guthrie Ferguson is a professor of law at the University of the District of Columbia (UDC) David A. Clarke School of Law and author of *The Rise of Big Data Policing: Surveillance, Race, and the Future of Law Enforcement* (NYU Press 2017).

Professor Ferguson teaches and writes in the area of criminal law, criminal procedure, and evidence. He is a national expert on juries, predictive policing, and the Fourth Amendment.

His articles have appeared in the *University of Pennsylvania Law Review*, the *California Law Review*, the *Cornell Law Review*, the *Minnesota Law Review*, the *Northwestern Law Review*, the *Vanderbilt Law Review*, the *University of Southern California Law Review*, the *Notre Dame Law Review*, and the *Emory Law Journal*, among others.

Professor Ferguson's recent book *The Rise of Big Data Policing: Surveillance, Race, and the Future of Law Enforcement* (NYU Press) examines how surveillance technology and predictive analytics shapes modern policing. Professor Ferguson's first book, *Why Jury Duty Matters: A Citizen's Guide to Constitutional Action* (NYU Press), is the first book written for jurors on jury duty. He stars in the "Welcome to Jury Duty Video" in D.C. Superior Court, seen by more than 30,000 citizens annually.

His legal commentary has been featured in numerous media outlets, including CNN, NPR, the *New York Times*, *The Economist*, the *Washington Post, Time, USA Today*, the *ABA Journal, The Atlantic* (digital), *Huffington Post*, and other national and international newspapers, magazines, and media sites.

Professor Ferguson serves as a Senior Visiting Fellow at the Harvard Law School's Criminal Justice Policy Program. He also serves as a Policing Data Fellow at the NYU Law School's Policing Project. Both projects focus on examining the civil rights, privacy, and public safety aspects of new surveillance technologies.

Professor Ferguson was voted "Professor of the Year" several times by the student body, and in 2016, he received a universitywide Certificate of Commendation for his teaching and service.

Prior to joining the law faculty, Professor Ferguson worked as a supervising attorney at the Public Defender Service for the District of Columbia. As a public defender for seven years, he represented adults and juveniles in serious felony cases ranging from misdemeanor offenses to homicide. In addition to participating as lead counsel in numerous jury and bench trials, he argued cases before the District of Columbia Court of Appeals.

Before joining the Public Defender Service, Professor Ferguson was awarded the E. Barrett Prettyman Fellowship at the Georgetown Law Center's Criminal Justice Clinic. For two years as a Prettyman Fellow, he taught and supervised third-year clinical students involved in the criminal justice clinic. Immediately after graduating from law school, he clerked for the Honorable Chief Judge Carolyn Dineen King of the US Court of Appeals for the Fifth Circuit.

Professor Ferguson is involved in developing constitutional education projects in the Washington, D.C., area. He is co-author of *Youth Justice in America* (CQ Press 2005, 2014), a textbook for high school students on their rights under the Fourth, Fifth, Sixth, and Eighth Amendments to the United States Constitution. He is on the board of directors of the Free Minds Book Club & Writing Workshop, a nonprofit organization that teaches creative writing and poetry to juvenile defendants charged as adults in the District of Columbia.

He holds an LL.M from Georgetown Law Center (Masters in Advocacy), a JD from the University of Pennsylvania School of Law (summa cum laude) and a BA from Williams College (cum laude).

Christina Franken

Christina Franken is project lead for the Mapbox Cities program. Trained as an architect and researcher, she works at the intersection of data analysis, urban tech, and user psychology. In her work, she questions how technology can and should influence urban space and what role open and closed systems will play in future smart cities. She also investigates how the people of a city can contribute to their urban environment to proactively influence how it changes over time.

As project lead for the Mapbox Cities program, she works with global partner cities on data-driven, open-source solutions addressing local and global challenges, ranging from traffic safety to behavior change to IoT systems to disaster response.

Prior to joining Mapbox, she was responsible for partnerships at Human.co, exploring how data can be utilized to improve the urban environment, so that more people choose active modes of transport, motivating users worldwide to be more active. During this time, her team analyzed and visualized data on human activity in 900 cities worldwide in real time.

To Franken, the needs of people should be at the heart of any smart-city project. She believes that only transparent urban tech solutions and interventions can be effective in making a city "smarter." Open-by-default systems and an open dialogue among stakeholders in the city are key, especially for issues, such as data collection and public-private partnerships.

Franken graduated from the Karlsruhe Institute of Technology in Germany as an architect and holds an MA from Central Saint Martins College (London, UK). She currently lives in Amsterdam.

Alexander Gelsin

Alexander Gelsin, PhD, is a founder and managing partner of bee smart city. He is an expert in project and product management, strategic product development, data analysis, and modeling. Prior to co-founding bee smart city, Alexander worked for leading financial services, fintech, and insurance companies in product development and smart-data analysis.

Alexander is a smart-city enthusiast, believing that new technology and data and their purpose-oriented and need-based application will help to make cities and communities more sustainable and resilient, and will benefit all stakeholders as the results of this application transform into collective good. He applies his technical and data-analysis expertise to assess smart cities and to provide implementation recommendations to improve smart-city development as part of bee smart city's holistic approach.

He holds a doctorate in physics from the University of Heidelberg, where he conducted research in galaxy cluster detection.

He is fluent in German, English, and Russian.

Bart Gorynski

Bart Gorynski is a founder and managing partner of bee smart city, which he co-founded in 2017. As a smart-city visionary, he defines a smart city as an ecosystem of smart-city solutions and has taken on the task of simplifying the smart-city business. Bart is a champion of the digital transformation of cities and communities and a fighter for future generations. He currently holds a number of visiting academic positions on smart cities at the EBZ Business School in Bochum and at the IREBS Institute at the University of Regensburg, both in Germany.

Bart has over 10 years of experience in the real estate sector, in open and collaborative innovation strategies, and in corporate strategy and consulting, and has enjoyed stays at Harvard University (US), the University of Regensburg/IREBS (Germany), the EBZ Business School (Germany), the Russian State University for the Humanities (Russia), and the University of Reading (UK). Just prior to co-founding bee smart city, Bart served as senior manager for Europe's largest real estate company, Vonovia.

He is a Certified Real Estate Investment Analyst and a Certified Real Estate Risk Manager, and holds an MBA in real estate from IREBS Institute at the University of Regensburg.

He is fluent in German, English, and Polish.

Pete Herzog

Pete Herzog is the shining example of a hacker trying to fix the world. He built a career out of taking the security world apart piece by piece to figure out how it works—but he still can't put it back together.

He is an avid and prolific writer on the topic of cybersecurity. He also writes frequently for the Institute for Security and Open Methodologies, a nonprofit research organization he co-founded in 2001. There, you'll find his work on the *Open Source Security Testing Methodology Manual*, Hacker High-school, and the *Open Source Cybersecurity Playbook*, as well as writings on trust metrics, authentication, social engineering, vulnerabilities, risk analysis, and many other security topics.

Herzog also teaches classes, coaches corporations on cybersecurity, performs security analyses for smart cities, develops security products, and advises start-ups.

Mike Holland

Mike Holland is executive director of the New York University Center for Urban Science and Progress (CUSP). He coordinates all of the functions and activities of the director's office as well as advising the director and other senior CUSP leadership to ensure the effectiveness of day-to-day operations and the optimal use of available resources. His role is also to provide leadership and direction for budget and financial planning, and to manage special projects and strategic planning.

Holland comes to CUSP with a background in research policy and the oversight of federal research programs. He previously worked with Director Steven E. Koonin as senior adviser and staff director in the Office of the Under Secretary for Science at the US Department of Energy.

Before that, he oversaw the US Department of Energy's Office of Science for a decade as a program examiner in the White House Office of Management and Budget, as a policy analyst in the White House Office of Science and Technology Policy, and as a Chairman's Designee for the US House of Representatives' Committee on Science.

Holland earned his PhD in analytical chemistry from the University of North Carolina at Chapel Hill and received BS degrees in electrical engineering and chemistry from North Carolina State University.

Kevin Fan Hsu

Kevin Fan Hsu is the co-founder of the Human Cities Initiative at Stanford University, where he teaches urban studies and international policy studies, and at the d.school. He was formerly an urban scientist with Walt Disney Imagineering, bridging the study of cities with sustainable infrastructure, energy, community mobility, and human-centered design.

He has been involved with a variety of projects in North America and in the Asia-Pacific region (including Beijing, Shanghai, Hong Kong, Singapore, and Taipei) and is a member of the Urban Land Institute's executive committee in Shanghai.

In addition to tackling climate change and urban development, he is interested in how valuing environmental sustainability maps onto efforts to protect heritage and promote cultural continuity.

He has earned degrees from Stanford in civil and environmental engineering, in earth systems, and in international relations. He has written on political and cultural affairs for *Foreign Policy*, the *South China Morning Post*, and Ketagalan Media.

Hon. Jerry MacArthur Hultin

Jerry MacArthur Hultin is the chair and leader of the Global Futures Group, a consulting, media, and financial advisory firm that supports the use of 21st-century technology to create smart communities and improve the quality of life of urban citizens around the world. He has worked with leaders and young people to encourage innovation, build smarter and more secure cities, and stimulate economic growth in communities in the North America and around the world.

Hultin is the founder of Smart Cities NY, a global smart-cities summit held each year in New York City, an adviser on urban innovation and infrastructure for the World Economic Forum (Davos) and the Global Federation of Competitiveness Councils, and co-chair of the Smart Cities Alliance for Malaysia. He has been a member of the Defense Business Board, where he produced a major report on the impact of automation and artificial intelligence on defense business processes and the defense workforce.

As an innovation leader, Hultin is an advocate and architect for hands-on programs that encourage invention, innovation, and entrepreneurship. As president of Polytechnic University, he helped create and develop entities, such as the Brooklyn Technology Triangle, the Varick Street Incubator, NYU's Cybersecurity Center, NYU's Center for Urban Science and Progress, the NYC Media Lab, and NYSeed (a public-private angel fund), as well as NYU's global network of campuses, including new campuses in Abu Dhabi and Shanghai. Hultin led the successful merger of Polytechnic University with New York University. From 2000 to 2005, he was dean of the school of technology management at Stevens Institute of Technology.

Hultin was Under Secretary of the Navy for President Bill Clinton from 1997 to 2000, where he was responsible for innovation and transformation; he also had a key role in developing the Navy Marine Corps Intranet (NMCI), which greatly improved the reliability of Department of the Navy communications and computing systems, and saved over $1 billion in annual costs. From 1994 to 1997, he was a member of the board of directors of Freddie Mac.

Hultin is a graduate of Yale Law School and Ohio State University, and served as a naval officer in Vietnam.

Jon P. Jennings

Jon P. Jennings is the current city manager of the city of Portland, Maine. He was appointed by the City Council on June 15, 2015, and assumed his duties on July 13, 2015. Prior to his appointment, he served as the assistant city manager for the city of South Portland. During his tenure as city manager in Portland, he has focused his efforts on right-sizing municipal government, so the city can concentrate on its core services. In order to allow the city to operate more cost effectively and efficiently, and provide excellent customer service, he has been exploring and implementing innovative ways to improve city services. His goal is to improve the city structurally, so it can have the resources it needs in the future to take on more aspirational projects.

Before to moving to Maine, Jennings worked in the United States Senate for then-Senator John Kerry, and held several senior positions in government in Washington, DC. Jennings worked at the US Department of Justice, where he served as the Acting Assistant Attorney General and Principal Deputy Attorney General for the Office of Legislative Affairs from April 1999 to June 2000. Jennings served as Senior Assistant to the Cabinet Secretary and Director of Policy Coordination at the White House from 1998 to 1999, and held a position as a White House Fellow in the Office of Cabinet Affairs from 1997 to 1998.

In his work at the White House, Jennings acted as a liaison to President Clinton's Initiative on Race, worked on Social Security reform, and served as White House liaison to numerous Cabinet agencies and the Office of the First Lady.

Prior to his work in Washington, D.C., he worked for the Boston Celtics for 11 years in a variety of coaching and management positions. He has served on the boards of numerous charitable organizations, including, in Maine, the board of Mercy Hospital, July 4th Portland, and on the City of Portland's Homelessness Task Force. He attended Indiana University

(Bloomington) and Harvard University, where he received his master's in public administration.

Ariel Kennan

Ariel Kennan is the director of civic innovation at Sidewalk Labs. She draws upon her experience in multidisciplinary design and technology to collaborate with community, corporate, and government partners to design service experiences, craft strategy, create digital products, and build capacity.

Prior to joining Sidewalk Labs, Keenan served the New York City Mayor's Office for Economic Opportunity as director of design and product. In that role, she led the design and development of a portfolio of digital products and founded the Service Design Studio, the nation's first municipal entity dedicated to making public services for low-income residents as effective and accessible as possible. Her time in government was inspired by fellowships with Code for America and the Center for Urban Pedagogy, where she discovered the potential for design in the public sector.

Keenan previously designed and produced experiences for the built environment, ranging from intimate immersive media to expansive buildings. She holds a BFA in integrated design from Parsons School of Design.

Matthew Klein

Matthew Klein is executive director of the NYC Mayor's Office for Economic Opportunity (NYC Opportunity) and a senior advisor in the Mayor's Office of Operations. NYC Opportunity uses evidence and innovation to reduce poverty and increase equity. It applies tools of research, data, and design to NYC's program and policy development, service delivery, and budget decisions.

He previously served as the executive director of Blue Ridge Foundation New York, one of the country's first incubators of social impact organizations. While at Blue Ridge, Matt helped create and build 30 new social ventures that collectively grew to provide services to several hundred thousand clients each year, and which had a combined budget of over $250 million.

Klein is a graduate of Yale Law School, Yale College, and the Boston Public Schools. He also serves as an adjunct professor at NYU's Stern School of Business, where he has taught courses on social venture investing and nonprofit management.

Martin Kõiva

Martin Kõiva is the co-founder and CEO of Qualitista.com, a software tool that makes it easy for customer support teams to give internal feedback to each other and helps them achieve a higher level of customer service quality.

After earning a bachelor's degree in journalism and public relations from the University of Tartu (Estonia), Kõiva went on to have a career in public relations, marketing, general management and customer support management.

Most recently, he spent four years at Pipedrive, a global maker of CRM software for salespeople. At Pipedrive, he built a team of more than 50 customer support specialists, who service 70,000 companies across the globe in two languages and from four locations. He also spent six months in Lisbon, Portugal, helping to get the local office of Pipedrive off the ground.

His articles have been published on the Help Scout customer service blog on multiple occasions.

Alan Leidner

Alan Leidner is director of the Center for Geospatial Innovation at the Fund for the City of New York. He has a master's degree in urban planning from Brooklyn's Pratt Institute and worked for 35 years as a planner and manager with New York City government.

Starting in the late 1980s, Leidner served as IT director of the Department of Environmental Protection, where he initiated New York City's enterprise GIS program and oversaw the development of the city's digital basemap.

He subsequently served as assistant commissioner in the Department of Information Technology and Telecommunications, in charge of the city's GIS utility. In fall 2001, he organized and managed the Emergency Mapping and Data Center, which provided information and mapping services to 9/11 responders.

After his retirement from city government in 2004, he consulted with Booz Allen Hamilton and worked as the northeast regional information exchange broker for the federal HIFLD to the Regions group.

In 2012, he helped coordinate the GIS response to Superstorm Sandy. Between 2012 and 2014, he served as president of the NYS GIS Association. He currently is president of NYC GISMO and is a founder/director of New York Geospatial Catalysts.

Leidner was appointed director of the Center for Geospatial Innovation at the Fund for the City of New York in 2017. In that position, he has been working on an underground infrastructure data interoperability project with the Open Geospatial Consortium.

He was a recipient of the 2001 Sloan Public Service Award and the 2002 ESRI Presidential Award, and was awarded a certificate of appreciation from the director of the National Geospatial-Intelligence Agency in January 2004. Among other writings, Alan's "Geo-Info CONOPS" article was published by *GeoWorld Magazine* in October 2007.

I-Ping Li

I-Ping Li is an innovation and technology evangelist and a seasoned technology strategy and delivery executive at Deloitte Consulting. He can be found advising and leading global clients on how to manage change through the adoption of disruptive technologies within their organizations.

He serves as the Retail Industry Working Group Co-Chair of the Industrial Internet Consortium (IIC) and holds an Information and Decision Systems degree from Carnegie Mellon University.

Josh Lieberman

Josh Lieberman is a senior research scientist at the Center for Geographic Analysis at Harvard University, working on hydrographic ontologies and semantic applications for the US National Map as part of the new Spatiotemporal Innovation Center. He also serves as a coordinating architect and initiative manager for the Open Geospatial Consortium and as a lecturer at the University of Maryland Baltimore County.

Lieberman has a PhD from the University of Washington, an MS from the University of Oregon, and an AB from Dartmouth College, as well as many years of experience in earth and environmental sciences and geospatial modeling.

Amen Ra Mashariki

Amen Ra Mashariki leads urban analytics at Esri. He is responsible for the strategy for applying data science principles to urban challenges, ensuring that data-driven decision makers will realize impactful and positive outcomes in urban policy and operations. Previously Mashariki was chief analytics officer for the City of New York and the director of the Mayor's Office of Data Analytics (MODA). He ran the civic intelligence center that allowed one of the largest cities in the world to aggregate and analyze data from across agencies.

Mashariki is an accomplished leader within government, the private sector, and academia, with experience in bringing big-data processing and analytics to large and complex data management efforts. He started his professional career as a software engineer at Motorola working on over-the-air data transmission projects, where he led a team of user-interface developers to build components of security features for hand-held devices.

Mashariki previously worked at the Johns Hopkins Applied Physics Lab as a computer scientist and research scientist, where he led a team working on data mining and data fusion projects in the bioinformatics domain. Prior to that, he served as the assistant director of informatics at the University of Chicago's Comprehensive Cancer Research Center, and taught computer science courses at the Hong Kong University of Science and Technology, and robotics at Northwestern University.

He currently serves as a fellow at the Harvard Ash Center for Democratic Governance and Innovation. He also served as chief technology officer at the US Office of Personnel Management.

Mashariki holds a doctorate in engineering from Morgan State University, a master of science in computer science from

Howard University, and a bachelor of science in computer science from Lincoln University. He is a Brooklyn native and attended Brooklyn Tech High School.

Dale W. Meyerrose

Dale Meyerrose is a retired US Air Force major general. Dr. Meyerrose is an international technology and cybersecurity strategist. As president of the MeyerRose Group, he consults with business, government, and academic organizations on strategy, digital transformation, telemedicine technologies, cybersecurity, and executive leadership.

He is a partner at RIDGE-LANE Limited Partners, a merchant bank founded by financier R. Brad Lane and the Honorable Thomas J. Ridge, former governor of Pennsylvania and the first secretary of the US Department of Homeland Security. He is chairman of the board of directors for Imcon International.

Dr. Meyerrose is an adjunct professor at Carnegie Mellon University, where he runs one of the very few cybersecurity leadership certificate programs in the country. He is an adjunct contract professor for the US Air Force, and a trustee and the treasurer for the US Air Force Academy Falcon Foundation.

Dr. Meyerrose was the first president-appointed, US Senate–confirmed chief information officer for the US intelligence community when it reorganized in 2005. Just prior to that, Dr. Meyerrose spent over 30 years forging a highly decorated career in the US Air Force as a difference maker whose innovation, skill, and commitment produced an enviable record of accomplishment. He served as the chief information officer for seven major military commands.

Dr. Meyerrose had major leadership roles in combating the early cyberattacks on government networks, in the creation of the early cybersecurity response centers, and in reorganizing new homeland defense architectures for the nation in the wake of the terrorist attacks on Sept. 11, 2001.

In addition to his distinguished military career, Dr. Meyerrose has won numerous professional awards, including the International Armed Forces Communications and Electronics Association Person of the Year, the Executive CIO Top 10 Leaders and Innovators Public Service Award for excellence in public leadership, and the Federal 100 Award given by *Federal Computer Weekly*. *Government Computer News* has also recognized him for outstanding information technology achievement in government.

He graduated from the US Air Force Academy with a Bachelor of Science in economics and holds a master's degree in business administration from the University of Utah. He earned a doctorate in professional studies in information management from Syracuse University, where his award-winning research focused on introducing new technologies to telemedicine. He graduated from the National War College and attended senior executive programs at the National Defense University in Washington, D.C.; Air University at Maxwell Air Force Base, Alabama; Harvard's John F. Kennedy

School of Government; the University of California at Berkeley's Haas School of Business; and the University of Virginia Darden School of Business.

Chris Moschovitis

Chris Moschovitis was born and raised in Athens, Greece, and moved to the United States in 1979, where he studied physics, computer science, and mathematics, and received his Bachelor of Science degree from the College at Brockport in 1983. His graduate studies at the University of Rochester and New York University included advanced courses in technology, management, and education.

After his move to New York City in 1985, he was appointed director of academic computing at Pratt Institute, and in 1987, he was recruited by the O'Connor Group for the position of vice president of information technology.

In 1989, he started his own company, the Information Technology Management Group (www.tmgr.com), focusing on providing independent technology management expertise and outsourcing services. TMG further expanded its internet offerings in 2004 by investing in emedia (www.emedia web.com), an award-winning and internationally acclaimed interactive software development firm, forming tmg-emedia (www.tmg-emedia.com).

Moschovitis is co-author of the critically acclaimed book *History of the Internet: A Chronology, 1843 to the Present*, as well as a contributor to the *Encyclopedia of Computers and Computer History* and the *Encyclopedia of New Media*.

He is certified in both cybersecurity (CSX, CISM) and IT governance (CGEIT), and is an active member of ISACA, ISSA, IEEE, and AMA. In addition to his duties as chairman and CEO of tmg-emedia, Moschovitis personally leads its cybersecurity and governance teams and delivers cybersecurity awareness training and consulting to corporations worldwide.

He remains an active speaker and writer, delivering workshops on a variety of topics, including cybersecurity, governance, digital transformation and interactive strategy, business transformation, and information technology strategy and execution.

His most recent book is *Cybersecurity Program Development for Business: The Essential Planning Guide* (Wiley, 2018).

Thomas Müller

Thomas Müller is a founder and managing partner of bee smart city. Prior to co-founding bee smart city, Müller worked for 15 years in state, regional, and local economic development organizations. In 2016, he represented the city of Mülheim an der Ruhr, which was named a Top7 Intelligent Communities of the Year by the Intelligent Community Forum.

With his deep knowledge of the public sector, Müller recognized early on the need for holistic and human-centric approaches to developing smart cities. In his years working for government organizations, he developed and implemented projects in diverse smart-city areas as catalysts for innovation and collaboration.

Müller holds an MA in economic geography from RWTH Aachen University and earned an MBA in international strategy and sales management from the University of Applied Sciences in Economics and Management, Essen.

He is fluent in German and English.

Emma Mulqueeny

Emma Mulqueeny is the founder of Rewired State and Young Rewired State, a commissioner for the Speaker's Commission on Digital Democracy, and a Google Fellow. She currently works with Her Majesty's Courts and Tribunal Service on its digital transformation program and as an adjunct for Ashridge Executive Business School.

She was recognized with an OBE on the Queen's 90th birthday honors list for services to technology and education and is included in the annual edition of *Who's Who*. Mulqueeny was voted onto the Wired 100, Tech City 100, and BIMA Hot 100 lists. She was named one of the UK's Top 100 most compassionate business leaders (*Salt Magazine*), one of the Top 10 women in technology by the *Guardian*, and one of the Top 5 influential women in IT by *InformationWeek*. She was also listed among the Top 10 Tech Heroes for Good by Nesta, the 25 most influential women in IT by *Computer Weekly*, and 2014's 50 most incredible women in STEM.

Mulqueeny writes regularly for the British press and on her own blog, and is featured on radio and television. She is best known for her campaign Year 8 Is Too Late, which encourages girls to engage with technology subjects, and her insights into the 97ers, the social digital generation.

Joseph Okpaku

Joseph Okpaku is the vice president of government relations at Lyft. He oversees a team of over 30 people, who have helped to create and implement, in less than four years, a nationwide legislative and regulatory framework for the ridesharing industry, including legislation in over 40 states and numerous municipalities. The Lyft Government Relations team has also been a leader in helping shape the creation of autonomous vehicle policy, with a focus on the key role that ridesharing will play in the testing, deployment, and adoption of AV technology.

Okpaku has testified before the Senate Committee on Commerce, Science, and Transportation, as well as the House Energy and Commerce Committee's Subcommittee on Digital Commerce and Consumer Protection on the role that ridesharing has to play in the coming AV revolution.

Prior to joining Lyft's Government Relations team, Okpaku served as chief of staff for Councilmember Ash Kalra in San Jose, California. During his tenure with Councilmember Kalra, he advised on all policy matters, including the development and implementation of a first of its kind land-use ordinance limiting the growth of payday lending businesses and an ordinance banning smoking in outdoor dining areas. Okpaku also advised on political strategy, oversaw media communications, and coordinated responses to all constituent concerns.

A native New Yorker, Okpaku worked for the Division of Enforcement at the New York Stock Exchange's Regulation Department for six years, where he investigated large-scale trading violations by member firms. He also spent over four years as an assistant district attorney specializing in prosecuting domestic violence crimes in the Manhattan District Attorney's office under Robert Morgenthau.

Gala Pin

Gala Pin is a district councillor for Ciutat Vella and Councillor of Participation and Districts on the Barcelona City Council, where she represents the coalition *Barcelona en Comú* (Barcelona in Common).

With a degree in philosophy, she has worked for the third sector and is a specialist in digital communications. She has been an activist for open software and network freedom, and the implementation of techno-political practices and digital democracy.

Pin was a member of the 15M movement in Barcelona, which called for rights to the city and rights to housing, and part of the anti-evictions struggle through the PAH platform (*Plataforma de Afectadospor la Hipoteca*, or the Platform Affected by Mortgage).

She has been active in the local movements of La Barceloneta neighborhood, participating in the recovery of the cooperative memory, the defense of a citizen port, and the movement against predatory tourism.

Jake Porway

Jake Porway is founder and executive director of DataKind, a global nonprofit that brings together high-impact organizations with leading data scientists to use data science in the service of humanity.

Porway is a machine-learning and technology enthusiast who loves nothing more than seeing good values in data. He founded DataKind in the hope of creating a world in which every social organization has access to data capacity to better serve humanity. He most recently served as data scientist for the *New York Times* R&D Lab and remains an active member of the data science community.

He holds a BS in computer science from Columbia University and an MS and a PhD in statistics from UCLA.

Vijay Raja

Vijay Raja is the solutions marketing lead for IoT at Cloudera, and is responsible for rolling out new and innovative solutions and use cases around IoT. As part of this role, he works with some of Cloudera's leading customers and partners globally to promote and evangelize IoT offerings.

Raja brings more than 15 years of experience in marketing, presales, and business development in the IT sector. Prior to joining Cloudera, he spent 10 years at Amdocs Inc., where he was involved in taking market solutions and services to leading communication service providers.

He has a bachelor's degree in engineering from the National Institute of Technology, Rourkela, and a master's in business administration from the Fisher College of Business at Ohio State University.

Jennifer Robinson

As director of local government solutions for SAS, Jennifer Robinson helps cities use analytics to turn data into information, so they are able to make more knowledge-based decisions, be more efficient, and serve their citizens more effectively.

Robinson's work at SAS combines her primary interests: cutting-edge software solutions and excellence in local governance. Throughout her career, she has participated in all phases of the software development lifecycle and has designed and assisted in the integration of corporate and government databases.

She has served as a councilwoman for the town of Cary, North Carolina, since 1999. Robinson has also served as chair of the Triangle J Council of Governments, and as a board member of the North Carolina League of Municipalities.

Robinson currently serves on the National Association of Regional Councils and for several nonprofit organizations, and as the chair of her region's transit organization, GoTriangle.

Jennifer Sanders

Jennifer Sanders is co-founder and executive director of the Dallas Innovation Alliance (DIA), a nonprofit public-private partnership dedicated to the design and execution of a smart-cities plan for Dallas. She brings expertise across a broad array of industries to the role, including energy, technology, economic development, and finance. The DIA's goal is to elevate Dallas as a city that is not only prepared for—but a driving force in shaping—the future of cities, and to provide opportunities for prosperity for its citizens.

While at the DIA, she has collated a network of 30 member organizations. She works with over 20 departments within the City of Dallas and Dallas County to accomplish an aligned smart-city strategy, beginning with the implementation of the first phase of the Smart Cities Living Lab in the West End district in downtown Dallas. The Living Lab incorporates eight smart-city projects into a compressed corridor, and the resulting platform will pull in startups, entrepreneurs, and university researchers to develop and test additional products and solutions. The Living Lab launched in March 2017.

She is actively involved with numerous civic organizations in Dallas and has served as the president of the Mayor's Star Council, on the board of the Suicide and Crisis Center of North Texas, as an ambassador for the Dallas Entrepreneur Center, and on the advisory board of Dallas-based retail and lifestyle start-up Edition Collective, among others.

She has been included on the *Dallas Business Journal*'s 40 Under 40 leader list, the *Dallas Business Journal*'s Top Women in Technology list, and the Dallas 500 influential business leader list, and has been named one of the Techweek 100. She graduated from the University of Virginia with a BA in psychology with a minor concentration in economics.

Eytan Schwartz

Eytan Schwartz is the CEO of Tel Aviv Global—an initiative aimed at promoting Tel Aviv as an international center of innovation by leveraging its status as the city with the highest density of startups and technological accelerators in the world, and as a leading urban destination for visitors, conferences, and international students.

Monocle magazine named him a member of its Dream Team of municipal officials. Schwartz resides in Tel Aviv with his wife and three children and has a BA in anthropology, summa cum laude, from Columbia University and an MA in Middle Eastern studies from Tel Aviv University.

Leah Shahum

Leah Shahum is the founder and director of the Vision Zero Network, a national campaign supporting cities working toward Vision Zero — zero traffic fatalities and severe injuries. The network helps communities develop and share best practices for safe mobility for all road users.

As a German Marshall Fund Fellow, she researched Vision Zero strategies in Sweden, Germany, and the Netherlands. Prior to that, she was the executive director of the

10,000-member San Francisco Bicycle Coalition, which promotes bicycling for everyday transportation. She formerly served on the boards of directors of the Golden Gate Bridge, Highway & Transportation District, and the San Francisco Municipal Transportation Agency.

Zohar Sharon

Zohar Sharon is the chief knowledge officer of the Tel Aviv-Yafo Municipality. He earned a master's degree in public administration and a bachelor's in social work from Tel Aviv University. He previously served as the municipality's social services municipal planning and information director, and later became chief knowledge officer of the municipality, among the first appointments worldwide to that post.

Sharon has won several national knowledge management awards, and as chief knowledge officer is in charge of all knowledge management processes in Tel Aviv-Yafo Municipality, for the municipal website, and for the municipality's digital transformation. He is also a digital leader in the national program Digital Israel; as part of this program, he helps municipalities in Israel carry out their digital transformation.

He created the DigiTel Residents Club, which helped Tel Aviv receive the 2014 World's Smartest City Award at Barcelona's Smart City Expo World Congress. Tel Aviv's DigiTel is a comprehensive platform geared toward enhancing civic engagement by facilitating a direct connection between the city and its residents. The endeavor has led to a profound shift in city government, making municipality services more accessible through information-based technology.

Sharon is a popular lecturer, giving lectures around the globe and helping cities to focus on practical ways to implement smart-cities programs by focusing on smart engagement with citizens.

Dave Shuman

Dave Shuman is an industry leader for IoT and manufacturing at Cloudera. He works closely with customers globally to help them successfully navigate their IoT journeys, deploy cutting-edge IoT use cases, and generate value from big data.

Shuman has an extensive background in big data analytics, business intelligence applications, database architecture, logical and physical database design, and data warehousing.

He has a bachelor's degree from Earlham College and a master's degree in business administration, information systems, from Temple University.

Kirk T. Steudle

Kirk T. Steudle is director of the Michigan Department of Transportation (MDOT). A registered professional engineer, he rose through the ranks of the department to his current position. Governor Rick Snyder appointed Steudle state transportation director on Jan. 1, 2011. He also served as state transportation director from 2006 to 2010.

Steudle oversees MDOT's $4.7 billion annual budget and is responsible for the construction, maintenance, and operation of nearly 10,000 miles of state highways and more than 4,000 state highway bridges. He also oversees administration of a wide range of multimodal transportation programs statewide. MDOT currently has 2,500 employees.

Steudle was the 2014 chair of the Transportation Research Board (TRB) Executive Committee and has served on the TRB Executive Committee since 2004. He also chaired the Strategic Highway Research Program (SHRP 2) Oversight Committee for TRB. He was president of the American Association of State Highway and Transportation Officials (AASHTO) from 2011 to 2012 and he has been a member of the AASHTO Board of Directors since 2006.

Steudle is a national leader in the development of connected vehicle technology, which allows vehicles to communicate with the road and other vehicles to improve safety and mobility. He continues to work with a partnership of governments and auto manufacturers to further high-tech highway operations and, at the same time, improve Michigan's economy.

Steudle was the 2014–2015 chair of the Intelligent Transportation Society of America (ITSA)'s board of directors. He is also a member of the Intelligent Transportation Systems (ITS) Program Advisory Committee to the US Department of Transportation. In addition, he serves on the board of the Engineering Society of Detroit, the largest engineering society in the country.

He also chairs the Michigan Mobility Transformation Center's (MTC) External Advisory Board (EAB). Steudle serves on the Lawrence Technological University (LTU) College of Engineering Advisory Board, and is a trustee for the Traffic Improvement Association (TIA) of Michigan.

In 2015, Steudle was named one of America's Top 25 Government Innovators by *Government Technology*. He received the Felix A. Anderson Image Award from the American Council of Engineering Companies (ACEC) of Michigan in 2013, and he was one of nine alumni inducted into the inaugural LTU Department of Engineering Alumni Hall of Fame in 2012. Steudle is the recipient of the 2011 P.D. McLean Award from the Road Gang for excellence in highway transportation. In 2010, he received the prestigious Thomas H. MacDonald award from AASHTO, recognizing him nationally for his continuous outstanding service and exceptional contribution to highway engineering.

Steudle is a graduate of Adrian High School and Lawrence Technological University, where he earned a BS in construction engineering. He also served on the Essexville City Council from 1995 to 1999.

Linnar Viik

Linnar Viik is a co-founder of the Estonian e-Governance Academy and program director in the central e-government.

He has been advising Estonia and many other governments on ICT and innovation policy and is recognized as an IT visionary. Viik has been instrumental in the rapid development of Estonian computer and network infrastructure, as well as Estonian internet voting and electronic signature projects. He lectures on innovation management at Tartu University.

Viik is a former executive at several mobile communications, broadband, and software companies, including Skype and Fortumo. He's been an adviser at the Nordic Investment Bank and board member of the European Institute for Innovation and Technology.

He is co-founder and member of the board of mobile services and software development at Mobi Solutions and Pocopay. Viik speaks English, Finnish, and Russian.

James von Klemperer

James von Klemperer is president and design principal at Kohn Pedersen Fox Associates, where he began as a young architect in 1983. His work ranges in scale from a house to a city, and he contributes closely to these efforts from conception to completion. In addition to focusing on his own projects, he leads the community of designers within the firm in exploring shared architectural agendas and goals. As president of the firm, he is responsible for leading the staff of 550 people in six offices around the world.

A major focus of his work has been to heighten the role that large buildings play in making urban space. He has explored this theme in major projects in Asia, including the

China Resources Headquarters in Shenzhen, Plaza 66 and the Jing An Kerry Centre in Shanghai, China Central Place in Beijing, and the 123-story Lotte World Tower in Seoul. In New York, his design for One Vanderbilt will link Midtown's tallest tower directly to Grand Central Terminal. Each of these projects creates strong symbiotic relationships between program space and the public realm. At the larger scale, his design for New Songdo City extends this challenge to the scope of urban planning.

Von Klemperer's designs have been recognized for the marriage of efficient program with adventurous form. His Peterson Institute for International Economics in Washington, D.C., Dongbu Financial Center in Seoul, Park Fifth residential project in Los Angeles, and Riverside 66 urban market in Tianjin have all received AIA design awards.

In London, he is leading the design of the Wanda hotel and residential towers in One Nine Elms. He is also active on the continent, in particular in Paris, where he is completing a building for the Ministry of Justice at the Parc du Millénaire, and in Lyon, where he is designing a series of buildings within the Part Dieu station precinct.

Von Klemperer has lectured at Harvard, Columbia, Tsinghua, Tongji, Seoul National, and Yonsei universities, the ESA in Paris, AMO in Lyon, and at Yale, where he taught as a Saarinen Visiting Professor. He recently spoke at the fourth Nobel Laureates Symposium on Global Sustainability, hosted in Hong Kong.

After graduating from Phillips Academy Andover, he received a BA (magna cum laude) in history and literature from Harvard in 1979. In 1980, he was the Charles Henry Fiske Fellow at Trinity College, Cambridge. He received his Master of architecture from Princeton in 1983. He serves on the board of directors of the Skyscraper Museum, the Storefront for Art and Architecture, as well as the Urban Design Forum. He is also a Trustee of Bard College.

ABOUT THE AUTHORS

Mike Barlow is an award-winning journalist, prolific author, and business strategy consultant. He is the author of *Learning to Love Data Science* (O'Reilly, 2015) and co-author of *The Executive's Guide to Enterprise Social Media Strategy* (Wiley, 2011) and *Partnering with the CIO* (Wiley, 2007). He is also the author of numerous articles, reports, and white papers on AI, machine learning, smart cities, ambient computing, continuous surveillance, real-time data analytics, digital transformation, and IT architecture.

Over the course of a long career, Barlow was a reporter and editor at several respected suburban daily newspapers, including the *Journal News* and the *Stamford Advocate*. His feature stories and columns appeared regularly in the *Los Angeles Times*, *Chicago Tribune*, *Miami Herald*, *Newsday*, and other major US dailies. A graduate of Hamilton College, he is a licensed private pilot, avid reader, and enthusiastic ice hockey fan.

Cornelia Lévy-Bencheton is a communications strategy consultant and writer, whose data-driven marketing and decision support work helps companies optimize their performance in the face of change. As principal of CLB Strategic Consulting, her focus is on the impact of disruptive technologies and associated cultural challenges that open up new opportunities and necessitate refreshed strategies.

She is a published author and career financial services executive, who has worked in the United States, France, and Switzerland. Her O'Reilly Media reports are consistently ranked among the top downloaded e-books offered by O'Reilly. Lévy-Bencheton recently worked on Smart Cities NYC '17, a "first of its kind" expo focusing on technology, urban life, and innovation.

She serves on the board of directors of the Financial Women's Association, as chair of the Strategic Marketing and Communications Committee, and as co-chair of the Emerging Technologies Committee. The organization's more than 1,000 members support empowering women through programs, mentoring, diversity, and education across the financial community.

She also serves on the board of the Data Warehouse Institute, a global organization whose members are dedicated to providing in-depth, high-quality thought leadership in business intelligence, predictive analytics, big data, blockchain, the IoT, and other new technologies through seminars, events, publications, and research.

Lévy-Bencheton earned an MA from Stanford University, an MBA from Pace University, and advanced certificates from New York University.

INDEX